Called or Chosen

The Awesome Life
Of
The Preacher's Wife
And
Women in Christian Ministry

Alice Palmer Hill

outskirts
press

Outskirts Press, Inc.
http://www.outskirtspress.com

ISBN: 978-1-4787-9427-1

Outskirts Press and the "OP" logo are trademarks belonging to Outskirts Press, Inc.

PRINTED IN THE UNITED STATES OF AMERICA

DEDICATION

"TO GOD, BE ALL GLORY HONOR AND PRAISE
FOR ALL HE HAS DONE."
And for placing the vision for this book into my heart,

To
"PREACHERS, THE PREACHER'S WIFE,
WOMEN IN CHRISTIAN MINISTRIES AND LEADERSHIP,"
For faithfully fulfilling God's Call

To
"MY PASTOR'S WIFE, MRS. TONY (JANIE) MINICK"
A loving, caring, Woman of God who is an inspiration
and blessing to me and to our church.

To
"PREACHER'S WIVES AND WOMEN IN MINISTRIES"
Who have shared experiences and godly
Words of Wisdom in this book.

To
"MY FAMILY, FRIENDS, AND CHURCHES"
Who have helped to make this book a reality.

To
"MY SISTER-IN-LAW, KATHY PALMER"
Kathy has a heart for God, for family, and for people.
She is a helper, giver, encourager, confidant, and friend.
A very special gift from God: to me and to our family.

Contents

Foreword By:
Mrs. Johanna Garrison

Johanna and her husband Doctor Alton Garrison ministered as evangelists for nine years. Later they pastored First Assembly of God Church in North Little Rock, Arkansas. She mentored minister's wives when her husband was the Arkansas District Superintendent. Her ministries changed again when her husband served as The Assistant General Superintendent of the Assemblies of God. Her book "Tangled Destinies" is most inspirational. Each time her role as a preacher's wife changed she prepared herself for each new phase of ministry.

Mrs. Johanna Garrison Writes

Alice Hill has provided mentoring through "Called or Chosen", an on-point book. She has brought together many godly pastor's wives who contribute by giving personal examples of situations they encountered.

Many of the chapters address issues and challenges that pastor's wives face but also remind us that with God's help and the empowerment of the Holy Spirit, we can make it.

Some of the topics are:

- Raising children in the ministry
- Dealing with unfair criticism and gossip
- Meeting unrealistic expectations
- Balancing family, church and work
- Church conflict and handling discouragement
- Personal calling
- Self-care how to maintain your personal spiritual fervor.

I have been acquainted with my friend in ministry, Alice Hill, for three decades.

She is an effective minister of the gospel and is a deep well when it comes to her wisdom and knowledge of God's Word.

She has a vast amount of experience as a former pastor's wife, evangelist, Children's Pastor, a mom, Arkansas District Women's Ministries and Missionettes Director and a passionate promoter of world missions.

I have always been most impressed with her deep love for pastor's wives, missionaries and their families.

This book will be a lifeline. The contributors are authentic and cover real-life topics most pastor's wives face. Wisdom and encouragement flow from the words of these women.

This book is a must-read for any woman in a Christian leadership role but especially pastor's wives. It helps them see that they are not alone in this journey.

Let this book encourage you and allow the Holy Spirit to empower you to become all that God has in mind for you to be.

Enjoy the Journey
Mrs. Johanna Garrison

Foreword By:
Reverend Pam Johnson

Pam and her husband, Reverend Bobby L. Johnson served as pastors and leaders in The Assemblies of God for over fifty years. They pastored First Assembly of God Church in Van Buren, Arkansas for thirty five years, until Brother Johnson was called to his heavenly home. Both had a heart for missions and Speed the Light, the Youth Ministry, providing vehicles and equipment for missionaries around the world. Pam continues in ministry as a chaplain, ministering to women in their darkest hours.

Reverend Pam Johnson Writes

There is nothing more powerful, than an idea whose time has come.

John 3:27, (John told his disciples that:) **"A man,** *(or a woman),* **can receive nothing except it be given him from heaven."**

For years, Alice Hill has been open to pray for and to share her own years of experience, pointing "Pastor's Wives and Women" in heavenly directions.

This book will challenge and encourage you to be strong, and to step up to the plate and fulfill your calling.

Enjoy your ministry
Reverend Pam Johnson

Foreword By:
Reverends Roy and Vickie Smeya

Called as God's Missionaries, Roy and Vickie have a vast experience serving as Assemblies of God Missionaries for over forty years across Latin America. Through those years, they have mentored and trained thousands of National Pastors and leaders, written leadership training materials and directed Bible Schools. Recently they have retired as full time missionaries. They continue ministering as God directs their lives.

Reverend Vickie Smeya Writes

For more than forty years I have known, loved and admired Alice Hill. She has put her heart and soul into compiling a book for Women in Ministry.

A welcomed addition for those who need a mentor, or wish to mentor someone else. It is full of wisdom that had come from her many years in the ministry.

As a pastor's wife, District Women's Ministries Director, and her Global Missions work, men and women alike will be inspired.

Reverends Roy and Vickie Smeya
Retired Assemblies of God Missionaries To,
Latin America.
Latin America Strategic Missionary Force, AGWM.

About The Author:
Reverend Alice Palmer Hill

Alice Palmer Hill enjoys over sixty years of ministry. Saved at age fourteen, and received the Baptism in the Holy Spirit with the evidence of speaking with other tongues. She was a Children and Youth Pastor, Bible teacher, evangelist, and musician.

Alice, her husband Reverend Billy Joe Hill and their daughter Debbie, pastored four Assembly of God Churches, evangelized, and worked in Youth Camps, until Bill was called to his heavenly home at age thirty-six. She and Debbie continued in ministry.

As an ordained minister, Alice served as the Arkansas District Women's Ministries and Missionettes Director for twenty-two years, on the board of directors for Arkansas Teen Challenge and Hillcrest Children's Home, ministered in prisons, in The American Indian Bible College, on Indian Reservations, on global mission fields, district councils, in Women's Retreats, and churches across the country.

Her book "I WAS THERE WHEN IT HAPPENED" highlights the outpouring of the Holy Spirit in the 1900's and the ministry of Dollie Simms who was ordained in 1914, when the Assemblies of God was formed in Hot Springs Arkansas. She preached for seventy-eight years and helped to pioneer thirty churches.

This book "CALLED OR CHOSEN" The Awesome Life of the Preacher's Wife and Women in the Ministry is a tribute to and a help for women in ministry: highlighting joys and woes of their lives. Some are "Called", some are "Chosen" to this high and holy calling.

INTRODUCTION: CALLED OR CHOSEN

THE AWESOME LIFE
OF
THE PREACHER'S WIFE
AND WOMEN IN MINISTRY AND LEADERSHIP

Revelation 17:14, "......... For He is Lord of Lords, and King of Kings: and they that are with HIM are, CALLED AND CHOSEN AND FAITHFUL".

This book is written, as a testimony of God's grace, His provisions, and His power. I trust you will find it refreshing and helpful to you and to your ministry as a Preacher, Preacher's Wife, Missionary, or a Woman in Christian Ministry and Leadership. What an exciting life we live.

Here are some words that describe the preacher's wife and women in the ministry.

Selfless, courageous, graceful, giving, help-mate, homemaker, leader of women, prayer warrior, compassionate, caretaker, caregiver, evangelist, husbands cheerleader, peacemaker, and one who encourages. She juggles time for her husband, her family, relationships, and her ministry.

There are mountain top experiences when everything is going great. There are also valley experiences when you may be tried to the very "nth" degree. However, every morning when you look into your mirror, say to yourself,

"Mirror, mirror on the wall, who is the most blessed preacher's wife and woman in the ministry? I AM IT'S ME! I like who I am, and I like what I see. Dear Lord: are You pleased with me?"

What an honor, privilege and blessing to be a woman who is called, chosen, commissioned, and committed to be a minister of the Gospel in these the last days before the coming of our Lord Jesus.

Whether you were "Called", or whether you were "Chosen" by our Heavenly Father, it is an awesome life we lead.

IT IS A HIGH AND A HOLY CALLING!

From the time we wake in the morning, until we fall asleep at night, we experience God's presence in our everyday lives as we follow hard after Him.

THE PURPOSE OF THIS BOOK IS TO BE A LIFELINE, of helps to encourage and strengthen women in their walk with God, whether married or single who are in Christian ministries.

It is written for pastors and the preacher's wife and to women in any area of Christian ministry, and leadership positions as well.

Please feel free to apply any part, or all, of this book to your particular life and ministry situations.

I have used many scriptures throughout this book. Hopefully they will bless and encourage you as you read each verse carefully not skipping over familiar scriptures: so you can apply them to your own personal life and ministry.

AS, "A WOMAN OF GOD"

I am changed, because my sins are forgiven.

I thank God for saving me, and baptizing me in The Holy Spirit.

I recognize that I am Called, Chosen and "Commissioned" by God Himself.

I am obedient to the role God has chosen for me.

My faith, my confidence and my trust is in Him.

He anoints, equips and enables me by His Holy Spirit.

His grace is sufficient. He is my strength, and my refuge
      My very present help when I face trouble.

He has called me to be: a woman of faith, integrity, purpose,
      compassion, wisdom and prayer.

I do not fit the world's mold.

I will model my life after the Proverbs 31 Woman.

My delight is in the Lord.

I am determined to follow where He leads me, and,

I am willing to pasture where He feeds me.

My goal and my plan is to follow Jesus all the days of my life,

So, when He comes, I will rise to meet Him in the air, and

I WILL ... dwell in the house of the Lord throughout all eternity.

AMEN.....

CHAPTER 1

SO! YOU ARE A PREACHER'S WIFE OR, A WOMAN IN THE MINISTRY, THIS IS YOUR LIFE

CALLED OR CHOSEN!

Whether you were called or whether you were chosen. Perhaps you are just beginning as a preacher, preacher's wife, or a woman in the ministry, or leadership.

Perhaps when you married your prince charming, he was a good Christian man. One fine day, he said to you,

"While I was seeking God about His will for our lives, He answered by calling us into the ministry."

Now, the last thing you would have dreamed about was that God would call you into the ministry. You really had not visualized yourself as "The Preacher's Wife". Perhaps you have struggled with this! Think on this:

When God called your husband into the ministry as a preacher, He knew about you and He knew your heart, your desires, your personality, and your abilities.

God did not just call your husband as a preacher, He personally chose you as well: to serve God as a preacher's wife. It is a high and a holy calling.

Or Perhaps: you have dreamed about God's plan for your life. You knew in your heart, that God called you to be the wife of a preacher or a woman in ministry. You prayerfully sought God's will, and for the companion He had chosen for you.

When God brought your prince charming into your life, you knew without a doubt that God's plan for your future had come to pass. Together you vowed to God and to each other that you would follow God wherever He would lead. Together, you dedicated your lives to follow God, and to minister the Gospel to all people.

SO, YOU ARE A PREACHER'S WIFE, OR A WOMAN IN MINISTRY.

Whether you are just beginning in the ministry, or a seasoned minister's wife, lady minister, or a leader in your local church: may you be blessed, encouraged and strengthened as you read the various thoughts God has ordained that I share with you.

There are "great times" and times we refer to as "bad times", times of testing your faith, your endurance, and sometimes your will to go on. There may be times when you are ready to say:

"I HAVE HAD IT"... BEEN THERE! ... DONE THAT TOO! ...

This sometimes happens on Monday morning, after a sleepless night in the parsonage when things did not go so well on Sunday. Remember God has promised that His grace is sufficient to see you through every situation.

Be encouraged, there will be brighter more rewarding days ahead. I have found that the good by far outweighs the bad. Remember you are human, and so are all those people you minister too. The Apostle Paul writes in:

> *2 Corinthians 12:9; "And He said unto me, "My Grace is sufficient for thee:" for My Strength is made perfect in weakness. Most gladly therefore will I rather glory in my infirmities, that the power of Christ may rest upon me."*

WHAT DOES GOD EXPECT OF YOU, THE PREACHER'S WIFE, OR OF YOU, THE WOMAN IN THE MINISTRY?

This may be very different from what congregations expect. It is likely that you may be compared to a former pastor's wife and expected to be like her.

May I recommend that up front, you prayerfully seek God, for the place, plan and ministry He has chosen for you in each situation. Thus, you can feel free and flexible to fulfill that ministry.

Know that there is no way you will please everyone in the congregation all the time. This is what I have lived by, it works for me.

"I will do my best to please God, and, if I please God, people will have a hard time finding fault with: who I am, and what I do."

DIFFERENT ROLES FOR WOMEN IN MINISTRY

There are different roles and different ministries for women in today's world. Your role in one place of ministry will likely be totally different from your role in the next place God chooses for you to fulfill.

You will likely wear many hats through the years. Some you will choose, and some may be chosen for you. Whatever your ministry, find that place of contentment and enjoy your life and, your role as a woman in the ministry. Highlighted below are various roles women are called or chosen to fulfill.

ROLE #1... THE WIFE OF THE PASTOR

As the wife of the pastor, you make your home a place of refuge and a sanctuary for yourself, your husband and your children.

As the pastor's wife, you may not play piano, speak, or teach a Sunday school class. God wants you to be comfortable with who you are with the gifts He has bestowed on you and what He has chosen for you to be and do.

You attend the regular church services. When the church has numerous activities and ministries, the pastor's wife may need to select where her involvement is most needed and satisfying.

You may sit on the second seat from the front; praying for your pastor husband as he delivers the message God has placed in his heart. You pray for those in the congregation to receive that word, and act on it.

You smile, you are friendly, you get to know and love the people. You listen to them with an open mind and heart. They will sense that you genuinely love them, and care about their needs and their problems.

NOTE: *God may place you in situations that will stretch you, and take you out of your comfort zone. So, be obedient, and not complaining, or fearful.*

He will not ask more of you than He will qualify you to accomplish. You may be pleasantly surprised what you can do with His help.

ROLE #2... THE ACTIVE PASTOR'S WIFE

You are active in the ministry. You may play piano, sing, teach and preach, lead worship, direct a choir, have counseling, administrative and delegating skills, the whole spectrum. Be careful that you don't overload yourself, which is so easy to do.

Remember, you are first a child of God. Your husband and your children are your priority, then your ministry to the congregation.

There may be qualified members in the congregation who have ministry gifts who can assume positions of responsibility. They can make use of their gifts and their calling to minister.

NOTE: *The Holy Spirit places individuals with gifts severally as He wills that the church may be thoroughly furnished and have a well rounded ministry to all in the congregation.*

1 Corinthians 12:11; "But all these worketh that one and the self same Spirit, dividing to every man severally as He will."

ROLE #3... THE PASTOR'S WIFE AS CO-PASTOR

You may serve as co-pastor along side of your husband. Your husband should take the lead. You may have many qualifications and abilities, yet you will want to be cautious so your husband, staff members or members of the congregation are not intimidated. If you have staff members, work as a team, each fulfilling their particular calling and ministry.

NOTE: *When and if, your staff and church leaders are successful in their accomplishments, growth and results, one must: guard against the feeling that, because they are successful in their ministries, that they will make you look bad. In reality, it is just the opposite: they enhance your effectiveness, and make you as pastor and pastor's wife* <u>*look good and even more successful in the eyes of the congregation.*</u>

ROLE #4... WHEN ROLES ARE REVERSED

When roles are reversed: you are the one who has received a call and anointing for a preaching ministry and your husband is the chosen one and will be a vital part of that ministry.

A word of caution here: use wisdom in approaching him as to how he will accept your call. Pray that God will reveal to him the place he will fulfill in ministry.

It is wise not to pressure him to make a commitment to follow your ministry. He will personally and prayerfully seek God's will and plan for him as the chosen one.

Your husband is the head of the family. You are a team, workers together with God. You are husband and wife first. Develop a working relationship for the ministry after that. He will likely have the ministry of helps and be supportive of you as a preacher. He will be a great and vital part of your ministry.

As a pastor, you are responsible for pastoral duties. Your husband will be a great asset, assisting with various ministries of the church. You are a team even when roles are reversed.

ROLE #5... THE PASTOR'S WIFE WITH A CAREER

You may have prepared yourself for a career and work outside the home and the church. Sometimes it is necessary to supplement the income for the family. It may also be an opportunity for ministry and outreach into the community as an extension of the church.

However, this should not be used as an excuse, for not taking your active place as, the wife in the home and pastor's wife in the church. There is a delicate balance to be kept between your place in the home, the family, the church, and on the job. You will want to make sure you have some time just for, *"THE PREACHER'S WIFE.....YOURSELF"*

1 Corinthians 9:27, "But I keep my body, and bring it into subjection: lest that by any means, when I have preached to others, I myself should be a castaway."

ROLE #6... THE SINGLE WOMAN IN MINISTRY

When God calls a woman into the ministry, regardless of age she is highly favored by Him. I am reminded of Mary the mother of Jesus, when the angel Gabriel spoke to her. She was a single young woman who found favor with God.

> *Luke 1:26-38, V28, "And the angel came in unto her, and said, "Hail, <u>thou that art highly favored, the Lord is with thee: blessed art thou among women."</u>*
>
> *V30, "And the angel said unto her, <u>"Fear not Mary: for thou hast found favor with God."</u>*

What a blessing and honor to hear these words. When God chooses to call a woman or a young girl into the ministry, He places His favor and a special anointing and touch on her life and desire to fulfill that call. The call may be as a pastor, a pastor's wife, a missionary, a youth or children's pastor, evangelist, worship leader, choir director, Bible teacher, or any other area of ministry.

Those whom He calls: He also qualifies. Of course, you must do your part, to educate yourself in His word, and in the mission He has given to you. Your success depends on how you surrender to God, and His leadership, your preparation, your attitude and your persona will play a vital part in your success.

As a born again child of God, and a woman in ministry we are the debtors. We are the ones who owe our witness to the entire world.

We understand that the world or other people do not owe us.

We are commissioned to present the gospel to all people, and lead them to a personal relationship with Jesus.

HOW DO I BEGIN?

This question has been asked many times. First of all, one must be saved, and baptized in the Holy Spirit: faithful to your local church, living a life style according to the scriptures above reproach, and know that God has called you into His service as a minister.

When beginning, start working in your local church under the guidance and leadership of your pastor and pastor's wife. When you share your heart with them, they will no doubt recognize the call of God in your life. They will help you develop that call and the gifts God has given to you. You may be asked to teach a Sunday school class, help in Children's Church, work in the nursery, Youth Ministries, or to join the worship team as a start.

NOTE: *As your ministry develops, God will open doors for you in the areas that He has chosen for you. At first, opportunities to minister may not be what you would choose, but walk through the doors God opens to you, as this will be part of your training and preparation for your ministry.*

IS MY ATTITUDE SHOWING?

Being accepted as a minister depends on your willingness to serve in areas opened to you. Your attitude and your demeanor will be an important factor in being successful in ministry.

If you have the heart of a servant, God will bless and great opportunities will open for your ministry. You will quickly develop a reputation whether good or not so good, this will follow you. Other than having Jesus in your life, your good name is the next best asset you have. Your attitude and demeanor will affect the success and the opportunities to minister.

NOTE: *Some ministers have felt that they should start out at the top, and anything less, is beneath them. Bad idea! Your willingness to be cooperative and appreciative of opportunities will help to open more doors for you. Learning to adapt to the culture, the program, and each situation is a must.*

I have been in ministry for many years and have <u>not</u> found it necessary to demand benefits or privileges. I have been invited into all kinds of churches and learned to adapt to whatever the situation required.

In a Native American church in Utah, on the Navajo Reservation, I was to speak through an interpreter. I was told that if it took me one minute to express a thought, it would take five minutes for the interpretation of that thought in their language. I had to make my sermon short, and to the point.

In this church, the little children were running around and playing during my message. The congregation was attentive to them, instead of what I was preaching. So, I changed my message to one on the children's level.

I chose a little girl and a little boy asked them to help me. I took them by the hand, walked back and forth across the front of the church, speaking to them, preaching on their level. I had the attention of all the adults. Oh yes, the other children sat down and listened. Basically I think they wondered what I might do next.

I was invited to speak in a church, when just before the pastor introduced me, he told me that the people did not like women preachers, and he was not sure of how he felt about them.

That's when I asked the Holy Spirit to anoint and give wisdom to minister in that service, *instead of being offended, I accepted the challenge.* The pastor's comments to others after that service was,

"We invited her to come and preach. We didn't expect much but were amazed and well pleased at the results of her ministry in that service."

Another time, a pastor invited me to speak in his church. Early that Sunday morning I drove across the state and when I arrived, He looked at me and said,

"What are you doing here?"

I reminded him that he had invited me to speak in his church on that Sunday. He told me that the youth had a program scheduled for that service. I told him that was okay that I would just enjoy the service the youth had prepared. He informed the youth that I showed up, and that they must postpone their program so I could speak.

How do you think I should handle this? When he turned the service to me, I asked the youth group to stand and commended them for their ministries, and for postponing their program. I thanked them for allowing me to minister to them in that service.

NOTE: *I did not put down their pastor for forgetting he invited me. That taught me a good lesson however, that, I should confirm the invitation before making the trip.*

You will no doubt experience all kinds of situations. How you deal with them will likely be a determining factor in receiving more opportunities to minister.

There will likely be times when put down, or rejection does occur. Everyone experiences that sooner or later. Even Jesus was put down and rejected not just once, but time after time.

He did not feel sorry for Himself, nor did He allow it to hinder His mission, attitude or His ministry: and neither should we!

NOTE: *Hopefully, you will "NEVER" take on the spirit of persecution, the spirit of put down, or even the spirit of rejection, because you are, a woman in the ministry.*

In fact, your attitude, and how you handle yourself in those times will likely detour this in the future. Respect your peers and those in authority over you. The apostle Paul said it well,

> *2 Corinthians 12:10, Paul stated,* **"Therefore I take pleasure in infirmities, in reproaches, in necessities, in persecutions, in distress for Christ's sake: for when I am weak, then am I strong."**

Do you ever have feelings of isolation and loneliness, or feel alone in a crowd? This can be discouraging and sometimes hurtful. Take advantage of your down time and use it wisely: call a friend; get your hair done, take up a hobby, get a pet or go shopping.

Spend some alone time with Jesus, allowing Him to have your undivided attention so He can pour His blessing, His direction, His guidance, His message or His assignment into your spirit.

As long as we are in our human bodies we will experience life's frustrations, situations and problems. We have the Holy Spirit to give wisdom, knowledge and the assurance that we are never alone, the Holy Spirit is always with us to encourage and help us.

Working with people can be the most rewarding, or at times you may experience your greatest pain. Just remember people who are not in ministry, have some of the same problems, and situations to deal with. So it is not strange that you experience those problems as well.

> *1 Peter 4:12-14, "Beloved, think it not strange concerning the fiery trial which is to try you, as though some strange thing happened unto you:"*

> *V13, "But rejoice, in as much as ye are partakers of Christ's sufferings; that, when His Glory shall be revealed, ye may be glad also with exceeding joy."*

> *V14, "If ye be reproached, for the Name of Christ, happy are ye; for the Spirit of Glory and of God resteth upon you: on their part He is evil spoken of, but on your part He is glorified."*

When I was asked to serve, as the Arkansas District Women's Ministries Director of The Assemblies of God, we had over four hundred churches in the district.

I decided from the very beginning, that any yes or any no decisions that the board members made about any of my ministry ideas, would never be about me personally, but would be for the good of the department that I represented.

It saved me from a lot of disappointments and hurt feelings through the years. I knew they were very wise, and that they had the success of the department at heart. It is not about you! It is about what is best and wisest for the position you represent.

There may be times when one needs a mentor. It is wise to carefully select mentors who have positive attitudes, and who are wise in various situations and allow them to help you through those down times, and times when you are hurting, or when you just need someone.

First, saturate your situation in prayer, seeking God for wisdom to work through your problem.

Building relationships with other singles in ministry, other ministry families, and other staff members can be one of the most valuable resources for you personally and for your ministry.

We are the family of God, and families help each other. Just make sure that those you confide in keep your confidences. And, those who confide in you can trust you to keep their confidences as well.

TIPS FOR SUCCESS:

- A recipe for patience: James 5:10-16.
- Planning: if you fail to plan, you plan to fail!
- To avoid stress, plan schedules and projects in advance, and in detail so you are always prepared.
- Live within your budget and your means.
- Avoid credit cards and debt.
- Be yourself, God will use you the way He created you.
- Allow God to use your gifts, and your personality.
- Dating: Be prayerful and careful in choosing who you will date.
- Every date could end up in a relationship and marriage.
- Dress appropriately and modestly,
- Your personal appearance is important,
- Remember you represent God and the ministry.
- Conduct yourself as a Woman of God and as professional.
- Always, avoid compromising situations.
- Place your trust and confidence in God, not in people.
- Develop consistent personal Bible study and prayer times.

ROLE #7...THE EVANGELIST'S WIFE, OR SINGLE EVANGELIST

This is a different life style for the evangelist's wife or for the single lady evangelist. You travel from church to church. You are in church nightly. The difference is: that you are here today and gone tomorrow. You leave the people to be mentored by the host pastor and pastor's wife.

You meet all kinds of people in all kinds of churches. Some experiences are good, some not so good. You do not get involved with the people on a personal or on a daily basis. The pastor and pastor's wife has that special place. It is best not to know the church problems, so your husband, *(or you,)* will be free to preach the message God gives for His people.

However, you may encounter pastors and pastor's wives, who may need someone to minister to them. God may have sent you there for them, as much as for that congregation. The Holy Spirit will give you wisdom to minister to them. Be sure, that they can trust you to keep their confidence.

Guarding and protecting the sacred trust placed in those who minister must be a priority, and must not be betrayed by repeating that which is shared in confidence.

1. **Churches make various provisions for their evangelists.** Some stay with the pastor's family as their guest.
2. Try to fit in with their schedule, so their family is not disrupted.
3. You will want to be helpful to the pastor's wife.
4. Keep your belongings neatly in place.
5. Clean up after yourself and your family.
6. Some churches have evangelist quarters, and bring in meals.
7. Others provide motel accommodations and meals.

Regarding finances: Pastor's usually receive offerings for the evangelist.

I recall a revival I preached in a small church. The pastor worried that the offerings would be very small. I told him not to worry, that God knew what I needed and He would provide.

That week, I had major car trouble. A man in the church fixed my car which totaled several hundred dollars. The pastor really began to worry. He was amazed: the offering for that week was the largest amount ever given to an evangelist.

The man, who fixed my car, had placed the bill for the car repairs, which totaled several hundred dollars into the offering marked: "Paid in Full". It really does pay to trust God.

A travel trailer is most convenient since you can equip it with personal needs, enjoy your privacy and time for study and prayer. The church will likely provide meals for you. Arrange your schedule so you have some down time to refresh, rest, and take care of personal matters.

If you have preschool age children, you may travel as a family. If children are school age, some evangelist's wives home school and still travel. They have classes until noon leaving the afternoon free for family activities, since they will be in church nightly.

Other Evangelists and Evangelist's Wives may agree that: she will remain at home with the school age children and enroll them in school. Sometimes this works well, and sometimes the total responsibilities of caring for the children, maintaining the home, and caring for daily chores alone, can place a strain on the marriage relationship and the ministry.

Sadly, there have been occasions when a ministry family has been broken apart.

Both you and your preacher husband made this decision. Should problems develop, together prayerfully evaluate the situation. Diligently seek God for His guidance and His direction as to what decisions are to be made. It may include making certain changes in ministries in order to guard and protect both your marriage and your ministry. Remember, your relationships are as follows:

    1st: Is your relationship with God
    2nd: Is your relationship as husband and wife, and family
    3rd: Is your relationship with the church

For years, ministers were taught that the ministry and church was to have first place. The church and ministry was given priority over the needs of the marriage and the family. Some marriages and families were neglected.

We nearly lost a generation of preacher's kids, who became bitter toward God, the church and the ministry. They felt, and sometimes they were neglected because the ministry and the church came first. If there was any time left, the family was sandwiched into it.

A Word to the wise: God placed you and your husband together, gave you a family and a ministry. He will require your spiritual guidance and loving care for both your family and your ministry so neither is neglected and both are fulfilled.

ROLE # 8...THE MISSIONARY'S WIFE
OR THE SINGLE MISSIONARY

You have accepted the call to Missionary Service. AWESOME! You have gone through the procedures and have received your Missions Appointment.

Now, you will travel to churches, ministering to the people, inspiring and challenging them to catch your mission vision, and, to raise your support budget. Finally your budget is raised, and travel arrangements have been made.

The day comes for you to say good-by to family and friends. You are overwhelmed with mixed emotions. You are excited about this phase of your life and ministry, yet experiencing the reality that you are leaving your loved ones behind.

I recall the first Missionary family I saw off to their new field. They had two small children. They said goodbye to family and friends, turned and walked down the steps to the plane, never looking back. I stood with that family as the plane took off. The Grandmother expressed her thoughts,

"It will be four long years before I see my Grandbabies again. I will miss their growing up and all the cute things they will do. The worst part is that when they return they will not know me."

I have also been with families and friends when a single lady missionary was leaving for her mission field. I witnessed the concern of her Mom and Dad for their daughter who was going so far away by herself, yet committing her to God's keeping.

I realized then, that the missionary was called, however, their parents, family and friends had not experienced that call. They were being left behind. Not only was the missionary sacrificing, their family and friends were sacrificing, maybe even more.

However, in these days, there are phones and computers that make it possible for both missionary and family to communicate as face to face with each other. This helps them stay close.

A Missionary's wife was so excited about all the people she would reach for Jesus. However, she found herself at home, changing bed sheets day after day, sometimes before the body heat got out of them so that the next guests could rest there. She cried out to God,

"I am just a maid, this is not what I expected and this is not why I came here."

The Lord let her know, that this was as vital and important as going out into bush country and reaching people. For, her home had become a haven for weary missionaries, pastors and families needing TLC, which she was providing.

As a Missionary, it is not always reaching large crowds. It includes maintaining a home without many comforts that we take for granted. It is ministering one on one, perhaps teaching in a Bible School, helping to pioneer a church, mentoring women and little children and YES,

Providing maid service and changing those bed sheets day after day. It is being in the perfect will of God and doing what He has chosen for you to be and do.

Recently a Missionary friend wrote of: how she felt when leaving one mission field, and accepting the call to another. She recalled how the people had ministered to them when her husband was so ill. Saying goodbye to those they had mentored and loved was like leaving part of their family.

Moving to a new mission field means: starting over again, learning new culture, customs and language. It meant packing up necessities, leaving or giving away things they could not take with them, yet realizing earthly possessions are just things, and that God will provide all that is needed for each new ministry He calls you too.

> *Romans 10:14-15, "How then shall they call on Him in Whom they have not believed? And how shall they believe in Him of Whom they have not heard? And how shall they hear without a preacher?"*

V15, *"And how shall they preach, except they be sent?"*

Some are "Called to go", others are "Chosen to stay, to pray and to send". What a blessing to have both financial supporters and prayer partners back home to intercede on your behalf.

NOTE: *You will want to keep them informed as to special needs and urgent prayer requests from your field. When you share your heart with them it helps to increase their vision for reaching lost humanity and compassion for supporting missions.*

When hearing a missionary share their call, I wanted to go with them. My first missions experience was in the country of Ecuador. My first time to speak through an interpreter I was concerned that I might say something offensive to their culture.

I asked the missionary to correct any mistakes I might make. He told me not to worry, that I could preach whatever I wanted to preach, because he had his own sermon. HA-HA-HA, It made me wonder, what we really preached. Anyway, God is the one who brought the results.

What an amazing experience. I realized how awesome it is to be called as God's missionaries. Think about being privileged to be the first to bring Jesus to a people who have never even heard His name, to nurture them and watch them grow and mature in the ways of God.

Seeing such hunger for Jesus, in the faces of the people made me want to stay right there and be God's missionary. I returned home to continue as the Women's Ministries and Missionettes Director for the Arkansas District Assemblies of God.

My longing for Ecuador, was so great, that I would cry for them even in my sleep. My heart and life was forever changed. I prayed that the Lord would send me back to Ecuador.

He let me know that, He had allowed me to go and see the hunger for Him, so I would be able to inspire others to be sensitive to His call to go and minister, and still others to stay and support in prayer and with finances. This was part of my assignment He had chosen for me. So for twenty-two years I did my best to fulfill my assignment.

As a preacher's wife, a missionary's wife, or a single missionary, it is vital that we are willing and obedient to go wherever God chooses to place us. You may even face some dangerous situations. Know that God is with you in that "THERE" place. He is your partner, protector, provider, and your security.

When we look around, we see that we have a mission field right here in America. There is so much hate, conflict, and turmoil everywhere. Millions right here in our nation need Jesus. One church has signs at the exits from the church parking lot, which says:

"YOU ARE NOW ENTERING YOUR MISSION FIELD".

Perhaps for some of us our mission field is right there where we live.

Are we willing to be God's missionary whether here at home or on some foreign field? Most of all, to be one who shares Jesus with those God brings across your path.

HAVE WE SOMETIMES MISSED OPPORTUNITIES? One Sunday night after church, we went to a small restaurant for a snack. A young couple was coming out as we were to enter. He held the door for us, and made comments like,

"Nice night isn't it?"

We agreed, and thanked him for holding the door.

He left to take his girlfriend home. On the way back as he topped a hill, two teenagers were drag racing to the top of the hill from the other direction. They hit him head on, and that young man was killed instantly.

The next morning we heard the news of the accident. We recognized the young man's name, and realized that God had brought him into our presence, he even opened the door for us, and started a conversation, yet, we failed to tell him about Jesus.

We missed the opportunity to witness to him. As far as we know he did not know Jesus as his personal Savior. Can you imagine how we felt, when we realized we had missed the last opportunity to reach this young man for Jesus?

We shed many tears over this; however it did not do this young man any good. It caused me to be more sensitive to those I come in contact with that I should share Jesus with them.

ROLE #9... THE PREACHER'S WIDOW

My husband and I had planned to grow old together. We were enjoying every day of our life as pastors of a loving church congregation when my preacher husband at age thirty-six answered God's call to come home.

After his memorial service, I shut myself in my room to process my situation, seeking God for what was next for me and for our daughter Debbie. My Mom came in and told me that the house was filled with people who needed encouragement. I thought:

"I know I am the pastor's wife, but how can I help anyone when I am so devastated myself?"

All I can say is that the Holy Spirit filled that room with an anointing far beyond my own strength and wisdom until the last person was prayed with.

The congregation was so loving and kind. They arranged for Debbie and me to continue living in the parsonage they had rented for us when we came as pastors. What a blessing. We did not have to be uprooted and move.

There were: thousands of dollars in hospital and funeral bills. I had no way to pay even one of them, because we had no life insurance. I laid all those bills out before God, and asked Him to supply the need.

People, some I did not even know, began sending and bringing love offerings to me until there was money in my hands to pay every penny.

God provided for us then, and after over forty-five years, He continues to provide His tender loving care. His love and care for His own, never runs out.

Someone told me, that the church was to take care of the widows and orphans. I had not yet faced the reality that I was indeed a widow.

The reality set in, when I found myself faced with decisions that I had to make for myself and our teenage daughter. There were many dark days and long nights, plenty of tears as I wrestled with the loss of my beloved husband and my grief.

Through it all, God was, and still is faithful! He promised me that I had nothing to fear because: my life and future was in His hands.

He assured me that: He was still taking care of me personally! To tell Him what I had need of, and He would supply it. Most of all, He would never leave me. He was only a prayer away!

He told me that it was okay to cry because He gave the tears as an inner cleansing and healing for my grief.

He spoke peace to my mind, heart and spirit and restored my joy once again.

WHAT A DAY! I had to come to the place where I permitted the Holy Spirit to be my comforter, and bring healing to my brokenness. Darkness left and my joy came in the morning.

One does not get over the loss of your companion, or any family member. You keep them in your heart, and in time, you adjust to your future, taking it one day at a time. I still have my times of missing my beloved companion, but the Holy Spirit is always there to fill that empty void.

One of my greatest struggles was dealing with the feeling that I was no longer in the ministry. Satan tormented me, telling me that I was out of the ministry.

The Holy Spirit reminded me, that I was in ministry before I met my husband and that I could trust God completely to direct my future. I knew in my heart what God had promised, and I took my stand on His word.

I knew that: **He had a plan for me, that it was to bless and prosper me, and not to harm me.**

Ladies, don't allow Satan to torment you! Let him know that you are a blood bought child of God. That the devil has no power over you, and when he comes against you, our Heavenly Father will deal with him.

In other words, resist him and he will flee from you because God gives His angels charge over you to keep you in all your ways.

God opened doors of ministry for Debbie and me. Pastors asked if I could teach a study course or seminar, or a VBS, Kid's Crusade, or preach a revival. I recognized that God was taking me out of my comfort zone, and would anoint and bless each open door for ministry.

When my husband was with me, I ministered under his covering. When he was no longer there, I felt the need for ministerial credentials. I followed procedures and was granted a license to preach from the Assemblies of God, later I was granted ordination.

The Arkansas District Executives, of the Assemblies of God, asked me to assume the position of District Women's Ministries Director. It was my honor and privilege to serve in this position for over twenty-two years.

Every situation is different. I have shared some of my experiences of how God provided for and took care of us in every way, so you will know that He will do the same for you. He is Jehovah-Jireh meaning God will provide.

May I encourage you to prayerfully seek God for the plan He has for you. Be careful not to allow yourself to sink into despair. ***God is still on His throne*** and, ***YOU are still His beloved***.

What now for you as the preacher's widow? Whether it has been some time or, recently that your husband was called home. You served side by side in ministry. If you were pastoring a church, the church provided a salary.

What now? You may be able to draw Social Security from your husband's account, especially if you have children at home. It may be necessary to find a job to support yourself. If you have been active in ministry, doors may be opened to you for ministry.

SO! YOU ARE A PREACHER'S WIFE OR, A WOMAN IN THE MINISTRY,THIS IS YOUR LIFE ⤷

If you have children in the home, they will need you more than ever. You now hold the double role of both mother and father, having all the care, provisions and decisions to make for each child. The Lord will give you a special touch, anointing and wisdom to comfort and guide them through their grief. Assure them that God loves them and He will always be with them.

You may live in a church parsonage. Finding another place and moving can be most stressful. If you have your own home, can you continue to maintain it? These are questions one has to face. Trust God to give His wisdom, His guidance and His provisions for each situation. Trust Him, He will not fail you.

A word of advice: don't cross your bridges before you come to them. Meaning don't torment yourself with the what if's and what should I do, or what should I not do? Make the decision when you come to that situation, instead of worrying what to do if this or that happens. The reality is: that those things are seldom the way you imagined they would be.

Your relationship with the congregation is totally different now. They will have a new pastor and pastor's wife ministering to them. The new pastor may invite you to continue attending the church. Sometimes this works well, and sometimes it places you under pressure to be on your guard not to infringe on the ministry of the new pastor and pastor's wife.

It is sometimes best for you to relocate to another church, so you will be free to become involved. There are so many ministries other than preaching and teaching that you can fulfill. Don't give up assembling yourself with the Family of God.

By all means give yourself time to grieve. I tried not to grieve, which was big mistake. The Lord let me know that grief was the process of healing when one experiences a great loss. The Holy Spirit is always there to help you.

The first year is the hardest, first birthdays, anniversaries and holidays.

At first, friends and family stay close, but after a while, they tend to think, if you can smile, or laugh once in a while, that you are over it. NOT SO, we are not over it. During the first six months, the shock of one's loss begins to wear off, and reality sets in. You realize that your life is forever changed and that there are a lot of adjustments and decisions to be made and, we gradually adjust to our future.

People may say things that upset you. They mean well. A friend told me that I should take off my wedding rings and put away his picture: forget him and move on. This was not what I needed or wanted to hear. Most people do not know what to say to comfort you. Their very presence is a comfort even if they do not say a word.

You may also notice that the couples you used to spend time with do not come around very often. The husband may feel uncomfortable, since his friend is no longer there for him to visit with.

Develop new friendships, perhaps with other widows. Go out to lunch, go shopping, take trips, pray together, study the Bible, and visit shut-ins. There are so many ways to touch lives, and make a difference as God leads you.

Get through your time of grief. Sadly I know some who have *remained in it* for years. Take heart, God will bring you through, and will restore your joy. You will continue to be fruitful for the kingdom of God. You have a lot to offer from your years of service and experience. Each morning when you get up, say to yourself,

"This is the first day of the rest of my life...
This is the day the Lord has made,
I WILL, REJOICE AND I WILL BE GLAD IN IT."

Do not be afraid to walk through doors that God opens for you. He will continue to lead and direct your life, even more so, now that you are totally dependent on Him. You have beautiful memories so keep them and your loved one in your heart.

ROLE # 10... WHEN PREACHERS RETIRE

Retirement: that is a time coming when we are to enjoy all the things we wanted to do but never seemed to have time for. It's a place where there are no schedules to keep, and no telephones ringing. It is the reason we have put away our nest egg, hoping it will be sufficient to live on in those *golden years.*

Before we realize it, ready or not, the thing we feared the most has come upon us. Family and friends gather to celebrate OUR RETIREMENT, and to send us off to OUR NEW LIFESTYLE.

It does not take long for us to experience the fire shut up in our bones and we find ourselves re-fired and back in action. Some I know have re-tired, and re-fired several times because the call of God is without repentance. *It is a marriage to ministry, till death do us part.* We may not serve as pastors or pastor's wives, but there is no limit to opportunities for us to touch someone's life for Jesus.

Find your place after retirement. Question is: where will you attend church? The new pastor will likely invite you to continue attending the church you and your husband pastored when you retired. Prayerfully seek God for His guidance.

Sometimes it works out great to continue attending the church as the *former pastors*. However other times it may create stress for you, your family, and for the new pastor and his family.

It will be quite an adjustment for you and your family if you choose to remain in the church you have pastored. Be cautious about visiting, and counseling former church members. Keep a good rap-port with the new pastor so he will not feel threatened or concerned about your relationship with the church members.

NOTE: *The hearts of the people must be turned to the new minister and his family so the church will be able to move forward under his leadership.*

Some ministers have found it necessary to enter early retirement because of physical situations. My heart goes out to them. I can relate with them. I know what it is like to prepare messages that God has burned into my heart, and to be unable to preach them. The fire is still there and it is shut up in our bones. *It is like we have been put on the shelf so to speak.*

I asked a preacher's wife who had recently retired because of physical problems, how she was dealing with it. She told me that she hated it. God's call is still in her heart. A retired missionary was going through feelings of no longer being useful or needed.

It is sometimes hard to understand why physically one is unable to fulfill the things God has placed on ones heart. If you find a solution, please, write it in a book, and send me a copy. *By the way, that is just what I am doing.* I am writing what God pours into my heart. I trust it will encourage and bless all who read it.

We go through different phases of our lives. You see, when one door seems to close, God opens another door, or another channel for us to continue ministering.

Perhaps God saved the best for such a time as this. Give yourself time to make the adjustment from FULL TIME MINISTRY TO FULL TIME RETIREMENT.

When Debbie was diagnosed with cancer, I could not understand why. She had served God her whole life, since she was saved when she was three years old. She had an active and proven ministry to children and youth.

When that door closed, God opened another door to her. Her ministry changed to one of helps for others who were dealing with cancer. She touched so many lives, and led several to Jesus. She could have given up, but she didn't. She never complained through all her suffering.

On Wednesday she was writing notes of encouragement to hurting struggling people.

Thursday the praise team from her church, First Assembly in North Little Rock, came and led praise and worship ministering to her and to us for hours.

Early Friday morning, God opened heaven's door and she entered her heavenly home.

Enjoy your retirement. Start your day praising God for all He has done. Ask Him to lead you through the day. Do what He places in your heart. You may be amazed what He has in store for your day. You may not be ministering to a whole congregation but there are people everywhere that need someone to minister to them. This could be a great open door.

For a while I was home bound, I did not have occasion to meet many people. I was annoyed because of telemarketers continually calling. Then one day God dropped something into my heart.

The next time one of those telemarketers called, I decided to let them talk a little then, I asked if I could ask a question. They readily agreed. I ask them if they had accepted Jesus as their personal Savior:

that Jesus was coming soon for those who were ready. I asked them, if they were sure they were ready for Him to come.

Some hung up quickly and some thanked me for being interested in where they spent eternity. Some praised the Lord and told that I had made their day. Some shared heartaches and their special needs and we prayed together.

WOW. Who would have thought that there is a whole evangelistic field out there among those telemarketers? Whatever role God chooses for you, whether you were called or whether you were chosen, be like the Apostle Paul when he stated in,

> *Philippians 4:11 " Not that I speak in respect of want: for I have learned, in whatsoever state I am, therewith to be content."*

NOTE: *Whatsoever state equals: the place or condition he found himself, he learned to be content. A POWERFUL MESSAGE don't you think? Focus On what we have instead of what we don't have!*

> *Hebrews 13:5, "Let your conversation be without covetousness; and be content with such things as ye have: for He hath said, "I will never leave thee, nor forsake thee."*

> *Jeremiah 29:11-13, "For I know the thoughts that I think toward you," saith the Lord, "thoughts of peace, and not of evil, to give you an expected end."*

> *V12, "Then shall ye call upon Me, and ye shall go and pray unto Me, and I WILL, harken unto you."*

> *V13, "And ye shall seek Me, and find Me, when ye shall search for Me, with all your heart."*

Give God your best, and your all, because God has planned a great life and a great future for you. THINK ON THIS!

HE'S STILL GOD!

No matter what I deal with.. He's still God.

Through my ups or through my downs...................... He's still God.

Of my mountain top experiences.............................. He's still God.

When I go through the valley experiences .... He's still God.

Remember, Beautiful flowers grow, down in the valley,
And so do we!

CHAPTER 2

PROTECT AND GUARD YOUR MINISTRY AND YOUR MARRIAGE

RESPECTING EACH OTHER IN PUBLIC, AS WELL AS IN PRIVATE

The position you hold is honorable and respected because it has been given by God. Your public and private life is on display. People are watching! By the way, God is always watching!

Some look for an excuse to justify their actions and attitudes. Others look for a role model to pattern their life after. When the world looks at us, do they see Jesus, or do they see those who draw attention to themselves? As ministers, our lives, actions, attitudes, and words must reflect who we are in Jesus. **We are:**

THE CALLED, THE CHOSEN AND THE COMMISSIONED, WE ARE, HIS MINSTERS.

Pastor, pastor's wife, women in ministry and leadership, you were placed by God to lead a congregation or a ministry. To show respect for the position you represent, it is appropriate to add Pastor, Brother or Sister before your name (*Pastor John, or Brother Jones or Sister Jane, etc*).

1111

This helps congregations to both honor and respect your position. You will want to be cautious about sharing too much personal information with your congregation. However, when you are in need, they can hold up your hands before God just as Aaron and Hur did for Moses.

Amalek and Israel were at war, Moses stood on the top of the hill with the rod of God in his hand. When Moses held up his hand, Israel prevailed, when he let his hand down Amalek prevailed.

> *Exodus 17:8-13, V12, "But Moses' hands were heavy; and they took a stone, and put it under him, and he sat thereon; and Aaron and Hur stayed up his hands, the one on one side, and the other on the other side; and his hands were steady until the going down of the sun."*

> *V13, "And Joshua discomfited Amalek and his people with the edge of the sword."*

Speaking of showing proper respect for those in the ministry,

I wonder: do we need to be more cautious about showing proper respect for the house of God? That is, for the sanctuary.

We do about everything in the sanctuary. Other facilities for activities are quite a different matter. I think about the time Jesus cast those out of the temple. He said in,

> *Matthew 21:13, "And said unto them, "It is written, My house shall be called a house of prayer; but ye have made It a den of thieves."*

Meaning that they were using it for everything else, after he cleared out all the stuff, He goes on in *verse 14, to say that,*

> *V14, "And the blind and lame came to Him <u>in the temple;</u>*

and He healed them."

Note: *The difference in verse 14, the blind and lame came to Him in the temple, AND HE HEALED THEM. There must be an atmosphere in our churches conducive to bring mankind into the presence of a holy and almighty God, because:*

THE WHOLE PURPOSE AND MISSION OF THE CHURCH IS: TO REACH THE LOST, AND TO PREPARE BELIEVERS FOR CHRIST'S COMING.

God is calling His ministers and His church to repentance and to walk in the old path He designed His church to follow. God is serious about what He expects from His church in these last days.

When entering the sanctuary, do we expect to meet and commune with God? Are we ushered into the realm of praise and worship preparing our heart to receive the message God has for us?

Is there an atmosphere where the Holy Spirit brings conviction to sinners, so they readily come to an altar of repentance, and receive life changing salvation?

Guarding the ministry, providing spiritual leadership for the congregation, who has day after day, lived in this old sinful world, and had to deal with everything contrary to the godly atmosphere of the church.

Guarding against becoming too casual is a must! This may seem like a very small thing.

When a pastor stands up behind the pulpit, <u>to speak for God to His people,</u> how casually he presents and conducts himself speaks to the congregation about the "Awesome God" he is representing to the people.

I am not speaking of being stiff and formal, **but respective of the awesome privilege of presenting the Gospel of a "Holy God" to His people.**

NOTE: *A minister will not just open a book of sermons and choose one! Instead, He spends precious time in the presence of God, praying and preparing the message that God is birthing in his soul.* **It will be a word directly from the throne of God for His people.** *The anointing of the Holy Spirit will rest on this message and the messenger and spiritual results will follow.*

We live in the last days before Jesus splits the clouds in the Eastern sky and calls His church to rise to meet Him in the air. We cannot afford to let down in even the smallest way. The souls of mankind are at stake. There is such a tremendous disrespect for everything in this old world.

How much more does the church need to be the church as Jesus intended it to be according to the book of Acts?

What should the world expect of us when they enter our churches? What do they see and hear? They are very perceptive of the respect shown for the minister presenting God's Word to His people.

They are very perceptive of the atmosphere among the people. If they should sense friction, or gossip, bad attitudes, discord, bitterness, or disrespect among the people, how do you suppose they will respond to the sermon and the altar call? They will likely leave without their spiritual needs being met.

I recall the testimony a famous evangelist. During the years of the Hippie Generation, he decided to dress as they did, to blend in with their culture, and went among them to reach them. He thought if he was like them, he could reach them. To his amazement, a large group of them came to him and told him they recognized him as the Man of God.

They further stated that, when they were ready to change their lifestyle, that they expected the church to be representative of God to them, and they needed to be able to look up to the church for an example of people who knew and walked with God.

They told him that they did not want the church to come to their levels, but to be the model they could look up to, that would lead them to a relationship with God.

WHAT DOES THIS SAY TO US TODAY?????

Oh, how vital it is that: those who are lost without God: sense love, compassion and a friendly atmosphere so that the Holy Spirit draws them into the very presence of God.

When the message is preached, and the altar call is given, they will desire what they see in the lives of the people and respond to the prompting of the Holy Spirit, accepting Jesus as their personal Savior.

A new name will be written in the Lamb's Book of Life, and a brand new child of God is born into the family of God. They won't leave there like they came! Thus your church is fulfilling its mission,

REACHING LOST MANKIND FOR JESUS THE CHRIST AND, PREPARING THE SAINTS FOR HIS COMING!

ADDRESSING EACH OTHER RESPECTFULLY

I have witnessed preachers and preacher's wives speaking in demeaning terms to each other, even arguing in front of church members and in public places. One minister was heard telling his wife she was stupid and calling her an idiot. What kind of example is this by men and women of God? This is unacceptable behavior!

Guarding our words, our attitudes, and the tone of our voice with each other, with staff, the congregation, the community, in businesses and in restaurants, remembering, people are watching your life. Be careful what they see!

NOTE: *Whether you are the senior pastor, youth or children pastor, or the pastor's wife, or a woman in ministry, you are a representative of God. What they see in you, will most likely be what you will see in them. Your congregation will rise no higher spiritually than their leaders.*

When going out in public and meeting people, I was aware that I represented God and His church, and was careful of my appearance, my attitude and my actions.

I did not want anyone who knew me to be ashamed, or embarrassed to meet me, or to introduce me to their friends or associates. This was not a matter of pride, but of respect for what and who I represented.

CORRECTING EACH OTHER IN PUBLIC

Walk softly! Be very careful about correcting each other in public. Make sure of your facts and message especially when making announcements or relating a story or testimony.

Have you ever experienced this? One person begins telling their story, and the other party interrupts to tell it their way. They sometimes end up in a public outburst of disagreement. If corrections are to be made, perhaps it is best to do it in private.

My pastor husband would occasionally stick is hands in his pockets as he preached, other times he would point down when speaking of heaven, up when speaking of hell and point his finger at the congregation instead of the open hand.

So, at home, privately, I shared with him, that gestures, can be distracting and encouraged him to please watch these things.

Question: *How do you feel when someone points a finger at you, and how do you feel if they extend their open hand toward you?*

Well, out of habit he would forget, and would stick his hands down in his pockets. *So, once again, privately at home,* I suggested that, maybe I should sew up his pockets so he would not stick his hands in them.

Well that didn't work either. So, I sewed up all his pockets. The next time while preaching, he tried to stick his hands in his pockets he looked surprised. He found that they had been sewn together. Problem solved! He stopped sticking his hands in his pockets.

NOTE: *Sometimes little things like using gestures, slang words or phrases distract from how others will receive and react to what you say and do. Satan will use anything to steal the word from the hearts of God's people.*

GUARDING AND PROTECTING YOUR MINISTRY AND YOUR MARRIAGE

Satan would like nothing better than to destroy your marriage, and your ministry. The Bible admonishes us to avoid circumstances or situations that could bring moral and spiritual downfall.

> *1 Thessalonians 5:22-23, "Abstain from all appearance of evil."*

> *V23. "And the very God of peace sanctify you wholly; and I pray God your whole spirit and soul and body be preserved blameless unto the coming of our Lord Jesus Christ."*

On one occasion in our ministry we allowed a young lady to go with us to our next pastorate. We set her up in an apartment, and helped her get a job. Word came to us that she was bragging about her intentions toward my preacher husband.

We decided that I should talk to her and warn her to be careful about her actions, what she did and what she said. She promised she would stop however she did not change. In fact, she was doing other things unbecoming a Christian.

After much prayer, the decision was made to take her back to her home. This was something we did not want to do. But for the protection of our lives, the ministry and the church it was deemed necessary.

Another time, two young ladies came to our church. They began flirting with all the young men of our church including my preacher husband. If they saw him driving down the main street, one of them would call me and tell me that my husband was just by her house, and that he would be home soon. They were continually trying to create problems.

After much prayer asking God to protect our families, our ministry and the church those girls left the church and the city.

There are sometimes those who come to seek out who they can trap. Satan will use anyone to destroy both your ministry, and your marriage. Be wise and watchful.

NOTE: *Please know that it is not necessary to have "the spirit of suspicion". God has provided Spiritual Gifts of Wisdom, Knowledge and Discernment among others, to be active in the believer and the church.*

These alert us when evil is present so we can take action and stop Satan's attacks from destroying our marriages, our ministries and our churches.

AVOIDING SATAN'S TRAPS

A young minister's wife told me how another minister was making persistent and serious advances to her. I warned her to tell him to stop, that she should tell her husband and together confront him.

They prayed for wisdom and felt led to resign their positions and left that church. God led them to another place of ministry.

NOTE: *Trust the Holy Spirit to guide you in decisions that must be made. Here are some recommendations to help avoid dangerous traps that Satan sets for you.*

- Guard against getting yourself into compromising situations.
- Be watchful of situations that could be misunderstood.
- By all means, trust one another there is no place for jealousy.
- When counseling a lady, pastor should leave office door open.
- Set behind the desk, avoiding any personal contact with the person.
- When counseling ladies it is best as a pastor and wife team.
- Guard your reputation, your marriage and your ministry.
- When praying for man or woman I use only one finger and touch their forehead as a point of contact.
- Pastor and pastor's wife do visitation together when possible.
- Pastor should have the church board, or someone he trusts with him when he is dealing with church problems and situations.
- Respect each other in all circumstances.

NOTE: *Let it be known that both you and your companion are devoted to each other.*

You may show some appropriate affection to each other.

This should discourage unwanted advances by others.

SETTING YOUR PRIORITIES IN ORDER

For years, ministers and their wives were taught that the church and the ministry came first. We nearly lost a generation of Preacher's Kids as a result. They felt they were neglected and many were. If there was any free time left, the family was squeezed in to it. *How sad!*

There were marriages and ministries lost as well. I am so glad we now realize that there must be priorities set for the preacher's family and their ministry.

FIRST: Your relationship with God must be your first priority.
SECOND: Your Marriage and Family is your second priority.
THIRD: Your Ministry and the Church is your third priority.

NOTE: This does not mean that the ministry is taking second place, only that priorities are being set for ministry and family so neither suffers. This does not mean that family hinders one's ministry.

Only that you recognize that God has given you your companion and He has placed those children in your care. He will require their training and Spiritual welfare at your hands just as He will require your dedication to the ministry.

There MUST be a ***balance*** between family and ministry. Neither one should suffer or be neglected. The Bible says in,

> **1 Timothy 5:8, "But if any provide not for his own, and specially for those of his own house, he hath denied the faith, and is worse than an infidel."**

DATE NIGHT WITH THE PREACHER

Taking time for each other is vital to your marriage and your ministry.

Set a specific time for you and your husband to go out on a date, maybe once a week just to enjoy each other's company. This is not the time to share church problems, visions, and your burdens of the ministry. This is a time you set aside for a romantic and personal time together!

One preacher's wife felt the need to spend quality time alone with her preacher husband *without interruptions*. She picked him up, at the church, and on the way home, she told him he had just been kidnapped. She had made arrangements in case of church emergencies, made reservations, packed their clothes, prepared special foods, had it all in the trunk of their car. She whisked him off to their special place for a romantic getaway. Good for her!

WHEN THERE IS A CRISIS IN
THE PREACHER'S MARRIAGE

"OH!" preachers do not have crises times in their perfect marriage! It happens! Sooner or later, every marriage experiences times of crisis of one kind or another. How a couple deals with crisis and problems determines the success or failure of their marriage and their ministry. When feelings are hurt or misunderstandings occur, deal with problems as they arise.

"NEVER LET THE SUN GO DOWN ON YOUR WRATH!"

Ephesians 4:26, "Be angry, and sin not: let not the sun go down upon your wrath:"

V27, "Neither give place to the devil."

NOTE: If you do, the next day your problem will magnify itself. The longer you allow disagreements, or problems to go on, the bigger they will become.

Remember, words spoken in anger can wound deeply. Words and attitudes can destroy relationships. Once words are spoken they can never be taken back. So, engage brain before opening mouth.

Mark 11:26, "But if ye do not forgive, neither will your Father which is in heaven forgive your trespasses."

There must be *FORGIVENESS* in marriage, in families, in ministry and in everyday life. To forgive is not a question of: whether or not one feels like it or if the offender doesn't deserve forgiveness.

**It is a commandment, it is a commitment,
It is a choice not to hold offenses against one another!**

This means, the next time there is a problem, one does not bring up past hurts, or old problems.

NOTE: *To forgive is a command from God. It is also an expression of your love for each other. Allow these challenges, conflicts and struggles, to draw you closer to each other and to God, as well as developing Christian character. Success in marriage takes mature love, commitment, compromise, understanding, and includes* **ROMANCE***! Being sensitive to the personal and emotional needs of each other is a must.*

Do those special little things for each other, instead of criticizing every little thing that bugs you: like <u>nit picking</u> every little thing which will continually annoy your companion.

KEYS TO FORGIVENESS

"I will forgive you, but I won't forget!"

Have you ever heard someone make that statement? The fact is, everything is recorded in our memory bank.

The secret is: when you forgive, you purpose in your mind and heart that the offense will stay in the memory bank, not to be brought out for any reason or on any occasion.

In other words, lock the door to that room in your memory bank and throw away the key.

Another effective key in forgiving is to spend private personal time in God's presence. Gaining power to overcome the offence, and release the person who offended you. You are then set free from bondage, and from an unforgiving spirit.

CHOOSE BETWEEN A TIMEOUT AND A BURNOUT

How many times have you heard someone make this statement?

"I would rather burnout for Jesus than rust out for the devil"

Why choose either one? Why not find a balance? Instead of a "BURNOUT" take a "TIMEOUT", *to rest, refresh and renew....thus* being better equipped to fulfill the challenges of family life, and the ministry. When ministers burn their life candle at both ends after a while, their candle is burned out.

This *can* happen to you! Since we are in these human bodies, we can become mentally, physically, spiritually and emotionally burned out. We find ourselves empty and unable to combat the fiery darts of Satan and the stress of everyday life situations.

To avoid burnout, one must recognize the symptoms, and take appropriate action. You may need an extended time of coming aside to: relax, rest, refresh, and renew spiritually, getting into God's word, not just for sermons or teaching study, but personally feeding the inner man or woman may mean a definite change of pace. In other words give yourself a TIMEOUT.

SPIRITUAL, PHYSICAL AND EMOTIONAL TIMEOUT

One of the best ways to be renewed and refreshed is to spend time in the presence of God allowing Him to pour into your innermost being.

Not always praying for wants or needs, but worshiping, praising, and waiting in His presence for direction, renewal and most of all to hear what He has to say to you. This is sometimes referred to as a Sabbatical.

A preacher and preacher's wife resigned their church, and became somewhat of a recluse. They had dealt with church problems twenty-four hours a day, seven days a week, for several years, as well as serious family, health and financial pressures. In other words, they were suffering from, and experiencing total *"BURNOUT"*.

They were criticized and accused of quitting the ministry. During this time, they took secular jobs from nine to five, five days a week.

They spent quality time together, time in the Word and in prayer, waiting on and seeking God to refresh their physical bodies, their minds and experiencing a spiritual renewal. They gave themselves a TIMEOUT, a Sabbatical.

At the end of the designated time, they quit their secular jobs and became very effective pastors, with a fresh vision, refreshed in mind, body, and spirit.

BURNOUT can be avoided by pacing yourself, recognizing the importance of taking a time out, and by waiting in the presence of the Lord for daily guidance, direction and wisdom. Oft times, we take on much more than what God has planned for us or even what God has asked of us.

WORDS OF WISDOM FROM A MAN OF GOD

We accepted the pastorate of a church with a partially completed building program. My preacher husband worked day and night on the building. He would come home exhausted and fall into bed, get up early the next morning and start again.

Meantime, we were in a revival at the church. He would stop work long enough to conduct the service each night. He was sacrificing his quiet time alone with God to refresh spiritually, his prayer time, his study and his sermon preparation time. He was burning his life candle at both ends. He was a prime candidate for *B U R N O U T.*

Does this sound familiar to you of your life style?

Our evangelist was Reverend Sherman Cox. A senior minister well seasoned, a very wise and experienced man of God. He called Bill aside and asked him if he intended to continue pastoring that church once the building was completed. Bill assured him that was his plan, and that he was trying to save the church money by doing all the work himself.

Brother Cox gave Bill very wise counsel. He suggested that if there were qualified men in the church to do the work on the church it would be wise to put them to work. If not, then suggest that the work be hired out to contractors.

He told Bill that by the time he finished building the church, he would be worn out physically and spiritually, that his ministry would suffer. That most likely the congregation would feel he was not fulfilling his pastoral responsibilities satisfactorily and would be ready to change pastors.

He related how the congregation would love and respect him just as much or even more if he kept himself as their pastor and the ministry of the Word.

In the Bible, men of the congregation were selected to care for menial tasks. This left the minister free to give himself to prayer, seeking God for wisdom, guidance and direction in preparation for ministry and spiritual leadership of the people which was his calling. The Bible deals with this situation.

> *Acts 6:3-7 "Wherefore, brethren, look ye out among you seven men of honest report, full of the Holy Ghost and wisdom, whom we may appoint over this business."*
>
> *V4, "But we will give ourselves continually to prayer, and to the ministry of the Word."*
>
> *V5. "And this saying pleased the whole multitude: and they chose Stephen, a man full of faith and of the Holy Ghost, and Philip, and Prochorus, and Nicanor, and Timon, and Parmenas, and Nicolas a proselyte of Antioch:"*
>
> *V6, "Whom they set before the apostles: and when they prayed, they laid their hands on them."*
>
> *V7, "And the Word of God increased; and the number of the disciples multiplied in Jerusalem greatly; and a great company of the priests were obedient to the faith."*

The results: there was an increase in the number of disciples, and the pastors (priests) were dedicated to the faith. The church grew in numbers and ministries.

Taking a timeout to evaluate how you spend your time each day is a wise decision.

Set priorities for yourself in regard to your relationship with God, your marriage, your family and your ministry so each will flourish and be fulfilled.

Chapter 3

WHERE HE LEADS...
I WILL FOLLOW!

OCCUPY UNTIL HE COMES

When we were first married, we were assisting in pioneering a new church. We had not yet gone into full time ministry. My husband Bill had a great job.

The president of the company approached him with an offer of training for executive positions in the company with substantial pay raises and benefits.

Bill advised him that he was a minister, and when God directed he would leave the company, to enter into full time ministry. Still he insisted on training Bill for as long as he was there. In the natural, this really sounded good to a young married couple.

Bill worked and trained in this company for the next two years.

The president seemed to think that if they could offer Bill enough benefits that he would forget about quitting and the ministry.

As for Satan, he will use anything to sidetrack one from following and obeying God. When looking back, I feel this was a real test of our sincerity for following God and the ministry.

Bill continued to work on his job and we continued to preach revival meetings and teamed up with Ernest and Ermel Hale. When we were not in revivals, we attended The Glen Carbon Assembly of God Church where Ernest's dad was the pastor.

During this time, God blessed our home with a beautiful baby girl. We named her Deborah after the Deborah who was a judge in the Bible, a wise woman who trusted and followed God.

God was dealing with our hearts to go into full time ministry. We received an invitation to serve as pastors of Clark Assembly of God Church in Northern Missouri. They promised forty-five dollars per week, and a parsonage to live in.

This was a long way from parents and friends and a giant step for us. We wanted to be sure it was God speaking to us. It meant that Bill would have to quit his good job, and depend on the Lord, and the church for our support.

You know how it is: you live and spend according to your income. We wanted to be sure we could meet our financial obligations. A preacher should pay his bills.

A good name is extremely important, if you are going to be pleasing to God, and effective in ministry. A good name is one of the best assets you have.

GO, AND I WILL BE WITH YOU "THERE"

We shared our hearts with our Pastor, Reverend Arlando Hale, and asked his wise counsel. He encouraged us to step out by faith if we felt in our hearts this was "God's Will" for us. That God would take care of us and provide for us when we were in that "**THERE PLACE**".

He referred us to **1 Kings 17:2-10.** Everywhere God told Elijah to go, He made provisions for him.

First God told him to go to the brook of Cherith, and "**THERE**", God commanded the raven to bring him bread fresh every morning and evening and he drank fresh water from the brook. The brook dried up, and God told him to go to Zarepath, that He had commanded a widow woman "**THERE**" to sustain him.

Our pastor told us not be afraid to step out by faith and go, because, when we were in that "**THERE PLACE**" God chose for us, that He would have provisions prepared for us when we got "**THERE**". In our hearts we felt God was telling us to,

"GO, I WILL BE WITH YOU, "THERE"!

By FAITH, We made the decision to quit the job, packed up and moved to Missouri. We combined our bills into one payment except for one item: My SEWING MACHINE. It was very important to me because I made most of our clothes.

When we got "THERE", things went well. God was blessing and the church was growing. Then, *"WINTER HIT"*. We had snow from early fall to late spring. Some weeks the weather was so bad that we couldn't have church. Finances went way down, some weeks we only received five dollars to live on.

It was so cold, that frost formed on the inside walls of the parsonage, like in a refrigerator. I did not have a washer or dryer so I washed clothes by hand in the bathtub. When I tried to hang them to dry, they would freeze before I could shake them out.

We heated the parsonage with oil. When it ran out, we would go to my Mother and Dads. On those occasions I did my washing at their house.

We would never tell my folks how bad it was, but they always knew, because God has given parents an insight on your behalf, that no one else has.

DISCOURAGEMENT KNOCKING AT MY DOOR

One day, a knock came on the door. It was a man from the sewing machine company. He said sarcastically,

"I am here to repossess your sewing machine, because you have not made your payments. You owe a balance of $110.00 and you have thirty days to pay this or you lose the machine. If, you can shake up that bunch of tightwads at that church you pastor you can get it back. Remember, you only have thirty days to get the money, or your sewing machine is gone f o r e v e r!"

He was laughing and mocking as he placed my sewing machine into his truck. He really upset me because he was repossessing the machine, and the remarks he made about our church.

When Bill came home, I was in tears. I told him what the man said, and how I felt. I was fearful that this would bring a reproach on the ministry, the church, and God. Bill reminded me about the scriptures our pastor had used and how we felt God telling us to,

"GO, I WILL BE WITH YOU "THERE!"

Bill just prayed this simple prayer:

"DEAR GOD: WE ARE IN THE "THERE PLACE" YOU CALLED US TOO. We need $110.00 in the next thirty days. We have no way of meeting this need. Our trust is in You Lord, and in Your Promises. Thank You for hearing and answering our prayer. AMEN!"

As we cried out to God, we felt a peace come over us even though we knew, there was no way that we could come up with $110.00, in the next thirty days. We only knew that we were, "THERE"!

Sunday at church, Bill asked the people to agree with us in prayer because we had a special need. We were not asking them to help us, just to pray and agree with us to see what God would do.

NOTE: *We did not tell them what we needed, because we were trusting God to supply it. Sometimes, we tend to tell what we need to everybody until someone feels sorry for us and gives us what we need. They receive the glory, not God. They also miss the blessing of hearing from God.*

A few days had passed. Bill walked to the Post Office to pick up our mail. When he came home, he had a big smile on his face. He said,

"Look at this, God has heard and answered our prayers!"

He handed me a letter. The envelope just had our name, city and state on it. It was a letter from a lady who had been saved in one of our revival meetings back in Illinois.

When I opened it, a $10.00 bill fell out in my lap. We read the letter together....

"Dear Brother and Sister Hill,

I was relaxing in my favorite chair, watching TV. The Lord spoke to me and said,

'SEND THE HILLS $10.00."

So, here it is! I don't know what you may need, if anything.

I Don't know your address, so I am just sending it to the town and state.

I hope you get this. I guess, if God told me to do it, He will see to it that you receive it."

Love Cordessa

We were praising the Lord, but then reality set in, I told Bill that this is a long way from $110.00 dollars, and the thirty days are nearly up. Bill reminded me of God's promise,

"GO, AND I WILL BE WITH YOU "THERE"!

SURPRISE, YOU HAVE COMPANY

We ran out of oil to heat the parsonage, so we went to my parent's house to keep warm, and do all our laundry. One of our deacons called and said,

"You have company from Illinois, a man named Jim, and his daughter. They can stay here with us, until you return home."

I said to my husband,

"I wonder: why has Jim made this trip all the way from Illinois?"

"This was not a great time for us to have company. The house cold, and we have no food in the house to feed our guests. What are we going to do?"

Bill, my preacher husband, calmly said,

"Sweetheart, we are going home!"

So, we went home! In those days, we did not lock our doors, since our house was a stopping off place for missionaries, evangelists, and who ever needed a place to stay.

When we arrived home, and opened the kitchen door, we could see through to the dining room. To my amazement, our table was filled with enough food to feed a fellowship meeting. The congregation heard that we had company so they quickly responded.

Now this was a sample of the love of our congregation, and most of all, the faithfulness of God and His provisions."

We rushed in, turned on the gas oven, so the house would warm a little, made beds, put down rugs and put away clothes. Bill called the deacon and asked him to send Jim and his daughter to the parsonage.

I MUST TELL YOU ABOUT "JIM"

He was saved in the same revival meeting as Cordessa. The night he was saved, his wife and six children came into the church service. She was crying. She said,

"We have to pray for Jim. He is out in the car with a gun. He told me to go on into church and when service started that he was going to take his life."

We immediately began interceding for Jim. We felt victory, and started the service. All of a sudden, the back doors opened and a man ran down the aisle and fell on the altar sobbing.

"Oh God, be merciful to me, a sinner."

This was "Jim"!

When Jim entered the parsonage that day, we greeted him and He said,

"I am here on a mission. Three weeks ago, God assigned me this urgent mission. I was afraid to tell my wife. Last night, God reminded me of the urgency, and that I should complete it with haste. When I told my wife, she cried and told me that three weeks ago, God assigned her the same mission and that she was afraid to tell me. This is what God asked us to do."

Jim handed my husband a roll of bills. My husband thanked him and asked me to entertain Jim, that he would be right back. He went into our little bathroom, and I heard shouting and praises to God. In a few minutes he came out, put the bills in my hand and told me to go and count them.

I went into the bathroom and counted them. There were ten, ten-dollar bills, $100.00 total! My heart was filled with praise. God reminded me of His promise,

"I SAID GO, AND I WILL BE WITH YOU "THERE"!
YOU ARE "THERE" AND I AM HERE"!

Sometimes we have to wait for the answer to our prayers. Even Daniel had to wait twenty-one days for his answer to prayer. The Bible says,

Daniel 10:13, "But the prince of the kingdom of Persia withstood me one and twenty days: but, lo, Michael, one of the chief princes, came to help me; and I remained

there with the kings of Persia."

NOTE: *God sometimes chooses to use people to carry out His answer to our prayers. They do not always immediately obey and carry out their mission. Thus we must wait, and continue to trust God for the answer.*

*<u>**Now if, and when God speaks to you and gives you a mission,**</u> know that someone is most likely waiting on God for the answer to their prayer. And, God is waiting on you for your response. So be quick to obey, and be part of the answer to someone's prayer!*

Sunday morning, Jim went to church with us and shared his testimony.

Sunday night, we related the story of the $110.00 dollar miracle. This testimony encouraged the people to step out in faith and trust God for miracles in their lives.

Monday morning, I called the man from the sewing machine company. I asked him to return my sewing machine. When he brought it in and sat it in its place, I opened it up and there was a sticker which read Repossessed!

Jesus had redeemed it for me. I realized how much He really cares about everything that touches our lives. Think for a moment: how He spoke to several people, He made ALL the necessary provisions and arrangements to fulfill the desire of my heart. He did it all for me in my "THERE PLACE" just like He said He would do!

I asked the man to sit down, that I had a story to tell him. I related how Bill quit a good job to come **"THERE"** to pastor that church. How we trusted God's promise to supply and provide for our needs, when He told us to "Go" that He would be with us when we were **"THERE"**.

I proceeded to tell him about Cordessa's letter; about Jim's salvation; and about the $110.00 miracle. His attitude changed, tears coursed down his cheeks. He said,

"I have heard of things like this all my life. I always thought they made them up. But I know this had to be God. I am the head deacon in my church. Our pastor has been trying to build a new church. I have been the one saying "No" that we can't afford it. After hearing this story, we are going to build that church."

NOTE: *When God's people obey Him, others are blessed as well. That church has been built. It stands as a testimony of God's faithfulness.*

I still have that sewing machine. Every time I open it up, and see that "REPOSSESSED" sticker, it brings tears to my eyes as I recall how God "REDEEMED" it for us.

We pastored that church for over four years. There were many times we reminded God of His promise for us to, **"GO, I WILL BE WITH YOU "THERE".**

Through the years, we learned that God always keeps His word. We learned to live by faith, and that we could trust God for everything we needed. I am so glad we obeyed.

When God speaks to you to "Go, or to Stay" He will be with you in your "**THERE PLACE**"!

THERE, is where He has provided the provisions for you.

THERE, is where He will be with you.

THERE, is where He will bless you,

THERE, is where you will walk in His perfect will for your life.

THERE, is where you will learn to trust Him, and His Word.

THERE, is where you make your needs and requests known to God even if it is as simple as the need for a new pair of shoes.

THE PREACHER NEEDS NEW SHOES

During those days Bill's shoes were totally worn out. He placed cardboard in them to cover the holes. He was embarrassed to kneel at the altar because he did not want the congregation to see that he had holes in the bottom of his shoes.

These were days when finances were very scarce. There were days when we prayed for food to put on our table. These were days when God taught us to fully trust Him, not only to lead and guide us, but to supply all our needs as well. Remember God's promise,

"GO, I WILL BE WITH YOU THERE"!

"THERE", we knelt beside our bed and cried out to God. We asked Him to provide a new pair of shoes for Bill. A few days later when Bill went to the Post Office to get the mail, there was a note in our P.O. Box, which read,

"Parcel too large for box, please call at the window."

He took the note to the Postmaster, and was presented with a box. He rushed home, opened the box, and there was a beautiful brand new pair of shoes, Style: Wing Tip; Color: black; Size 10 ½ EEE; The style, color, and size that Bill wore.

We wept before God with our hearts filled with praise. We had no idea where they came from only that God had answered our prayer and provided them. Once again, He had answered our prayer and provided for us "**THERE**".

Sunday morning, Bill wore his new shoes to church. One of our deacons came to him and asked,

"Pastor did the shoes fit?"

He proceeded to tell Bill that He was awakened in the night. God told him that his pastor needed new shoes. He told God that he would give the pastor money to purchase a new pair of shoes.

God told him, that he was to *get them*. He told God he did not know what color, style, or size to get. Then, God told him to get the catalog and to order the shoes. He showed Brother Carroll Hamilton the style, color and size to order. This was the same night we had prayed and asked God to provide a new pair of shoes.

> *Isaiah 65:24, " And it shall come to pass, that before they call, I will answer; and while they are yet speaking, I will hear."*

PLEASE NOTE: *the key to trusting God, is not telling anyone else what you need.....simply going to God with your request and wait for Him supply it, or to speak to whomever He chooses to meet that need, and for them to obey.*

We are prone to broadcast what we need, until those who hear it, feel an obligation to meet it. <u>This is not God's plan</u>. He will reveal to the one He has chosen to meet that need.

Then, God receives the praise and glory for all He has done and, they are blessed for being obedient to the mission that God has commissioned them to carry out.

Once again, God chose one of His children to answer our prayer. When God speaks to us and gives us an assignment or a mission, we know when it is God's Voice because we are His sheep, and we know His Voice.

You know that Satan will not tell you to do anything good. So when God speaks and asks us to do something, we must be quick to respond. Perhaps another one of God's children is waiting for an answer to their prayers and to their need.

DECISIONS...DECISIONS
SHOULD WE GO? ...OR... SHOULD WE STAY?

In our first pastorate, we were elected for an indefinite term. We began feeling that our ministry may not be as effective as it had been.

Have feelings and thoughts such as this ever troubled you?

We asked the Congregation to vote as to their confidence in our ministry. We prayerfully sought God's will for direction. In the meantime, we were contacted by the pulpit committee from a much larger church asking us to consider the position of senior pastor.

They promised a larger salary, and benefits including a brand new parsonage for our living pleasure. We consented to minister there in the Sunday services. They indicated that they wanted to vote on us in two weeks.

Now, the parsonage we presently lived in was a concrete block house with no insulation.

In winter, ice formed on the inside walls like in a refrigerator. Some weeks our salary had been about five dollars. Our congregation was very loving and did their best to provide for us.

What a contrast between the two churches. However, our main focus was, to be in the center of God's will, and to be effective in the ministry. I was not like one preacher's wife we knew, who in a similar situation, told her husband, "**You go pray, while I go pack".**

We spent much time in prayer seeking God's direction for our future and the future of the church. The question was:

"SHOULD WE STAY" … *at the church we were pastoring? Or*

"SHOULD WE GO"... *and accept the pastorate of the other church that had contacted us?*

However, no answer came!

TO FLEECE … OR... NOT TO FLEECE

We thought of Gideon, when the angel found him hiding from the enemy, and called *him a mighty man of valor, telling him that God wanted to use him to save Israel.*

In **Judges 6:36-39,** Gideon questions God's will: would He really use him and help him save Israel? He decided to put a fleece before God to make sure that God really meant what He said.

He would put some wool on the threshing floor that night, and if in the morning the wool (fleece) was wet and the ground was dry, then he would know that God would help him. God answered: the next morning the ground was dry and the wool (fleece) was wet.

Gideon still doubted God, So, he asked God not to be angry with him, and to reverse his question: this time, that the wool (fleece) would be dry, and the ground would be wet. The next morning, the wool (fleece) was dry, and the ground was wet. Once again, God answered and confirmed that He would use Gideon and would indeed help him to carry out God's Plan....

Gideon got his answer... This worked for Gideon in the Bible, and hopefully this would work for us. We decided to put a *FLEECE BEFORE THE LORD*. Since both churches were to cast a vote for our future, we decided this is how we will determine God's will for us. *THIS WAS OUR FLEECE...*

"God, if you want us to stay where we are,
Let the vote of confidence be 100%"
OR
"God, if you want us to go to the other church
Let that vote be 100%".

We thought this was reasonable, and that it would settle our dilemma. We will know whether we should go or whether we should stay. Both votes were cast. Would you believe?

<u>BOTH, OF THE VOTES WERE 100%</u>

We decided that a fleece was not a good way to determine God's will for our lives. Thus, we continued to prayerfully seek God for an answer regarding His will for us. This is how God answered our prayer,

He told us that He had allowed the other church to call and elect us with 100% of the vote. He also allowed the vote of confidence to be 100% where we were.

That He wanted us to know that our ministry would be effective wherever we were, as long as we stayed **"THERE"** in the place where He led us, and where His provisions were provided!

What a relief and peace of mind! We knew now, without any doubt that we were to stay with the little rural church. We contacted the other church to thank them for their consideration and that God had directed us to stay where we were.

The son of one of our deacons was the area presbyter where the other church was located. He asked his dad who they were getting for a new pastor. The deacon replied that they were not seeking a new pastor, since they had just given a 100% vote of confidence to the one they had.

The son revealed that their pastor had been elected to a church in his area. Our congregation realized that we had opportunity to leave, and chose to stay because we felt it was God's will and that we loved them very much. After that it was as though we were new pastors. The church grew from seventeen to ninety-nine in a town of about three hundred people, and three other churches.

After about four years the Lord let us know it was time to move on to another **"THERE PLACE"**. The City Council members came and offered to finance anything we needed if we would just stay. We thanked them, and assured them we appreciated their offer, but the Lord had called us to minister in another area.

The day we moved many tears were shed. It was like being at our own funeral. The congregation and people from the town lined the street, watching as each piece of furniture was moved. It was hard to leave them, but the Lord had released us. He was leading us to another **"THERE PLACE"**!

Ever feel like you are taken for granted? Perhaps you are discouraged, or have problems to deal with. You may be like we were, just wondering if your ministry is still effective.

Hold steady. Prayerfully seek God. **GOD DOES NOT HIDE HIS WILL FROM HIS PEOPLE!**

He will let you know, if you are still in that, **"THERE PLACE"** or, if He is calling you to a new **"THERE PLACE"**!

WHEN GOD SPEAKS BE QUICK TO OBEY

God not only speaks about His call on your life, there are times when He gives instructions you may not understand, as He did on this occasion. Follow His leading because He knows what is ahead.

In 1974, my beloved preacher husband was called home to be with Jesus at thirty-six years of age. Debbie and I continued in ministry as God opened doors for us.

We concluded a revival on Friday night and decided to stay in the area since we were to begin a revival on Sunday close by. All night, The Holy Spirit kept telling me that I should go home. It seemed foolish to make a seven hour round trip when we were already where we needed to be.

Saturday morning I told Debbie that I did not know why, but the Holy Spirit was telling me that we should go home. We packed up, and started home. We had not gone far until it began storming. It rained so hard we could hardly see to drive. Closer to home, we out ran the storm which seemed to be following us.

When we arrived home, we quickly knew why the Holy Spirit had impressed us to go home. The men of the church we had pastored decided to bless and surprise us with a brand new roof on our house. They were in the process of removing the first half of our roof, on the bedroom side of the house.

I thanked them, and told them they should cover the roof with tarps and plastic because a storm was headed that way. They quickly started covering the roof.

The storm came, and the wind blew the tarps off the roof, and the rain poured inside the house. The ceiling, walls, beds, furniture, carpets, and everything in my closets was soaked. Water was standing on the floors. People from the church came to help salvage what they could.

When I went inside the house, I met some people I did not know. They were in one of my closets going through boxes, salvaging what they could, drying everything with towels and moving them to the other side of the house. They introduced themselves. They were,

THE NEW PASTOR AND PASTOR'S WIFE OF THAT CHURCH!

Now, this could have been most embarrassing, especially if I had any skeletons or any secret things hidden in my closets, or anywhere in my house. You know: things that I would not want anyone, especially the preacher or preacher's wife to find or see.

Okay, Just to ease your mind! There were no skeletons or secret things hidden anywhere in my house. I am so glad, that I live what I preach.

Just a note: *just in case you ever have a rainstorm inside your house, be sure you do not have skeletons or secret things hidden that you would not want anyone especially, the preacher or the preacher's wife to find, or see! Remember, God sees all, and knows all!*

The rain continued to pour inside and out. My little niece Stephanie was a toddler. She started crying and said,

"The ole debil (devil) is in this house, I want to go home."

I told her to go into the other side of the house and ask Jesus to stop the rain. She went to the dry side of the house, in a few minutes she came back, and said,

"I asked Jesus to stop the rain, and He DID!"

I looked out the window, and just as she said, the rain had stopped.

Oh the faith of a little child. Never discount the faith and trust of children.

I am so glad that: I heard and recognized it was the Lord prompting me to go home. Glad that I listened and obeyed His voice and went home that day.

NOTE: *Just a thought, sometimes the voices around us are so loud, and so many, that it is hard to discern which voice to listen too. If our hearts and ears are tuned to our Heavenly Father, our Good Shepherd, we will hear His voice over all the rest, for His Word says in,*

> **John 10:3-5, "To Him the porter openeth; and the sheep hear His Voice: and He calleth His own sheep by name, and leadeth them out."**
>
> **V4, "And when He putteth forth His own sheep, He goeth before them, and the sheep follow Him: for they know His Voice."**
>
> **V5, "And a stranger will they not follow, but will flee from him: for they know not the voice of strangers."**

This is a testimony of God's blessing resting on His people. When we follow Him, He turns seeming tragedies into blessing. As a result, after the storm, my home was better than before. The homeowners insurance replaced the damaged goods, refinished ceilings, walls, floors and carpets, and I had a brand new roof.

> **Romans 8:28, "And we know that all things work together for good to them that love God, <u>to them who are the called</u> according to His purpose."**

NOTE: *Why, do we get all upset when things seem to be going wrong? When and if, we learn to trust the Lord in every situation, we can have peace in the midst of our troubles and our storms.*

While traveling with Missionary Nadine Waldrop, to the Navajo Indian Reservation in Utah, we traveled through a field to access the church where I was to speak. In that field, was a large herd of sheep and a large dog guarding and protecting those sheep.

As we drove through that field, the dog barked frantically and was trying to attack our car, biting at our tires. I noticed that those sheep continued to graze, they were completely calm. They had complete trust and confidence in that big dog to protect them.

Is that not a picture of the Christian when trouble comes, that we have complete calm, and trust that our Good Shepherd is in control, and we need not fear any alarm? Peace comes when we are living by faith and trust in our Good Shepherd.

WHERE TOO NEXT LORD?

When Debbie and I concluded a meeting, and if we did not have another meeting scheduled, we would stop at the edge of the city and pray. We would ask the Lord:

"Where too next Lord? Where do you want us to go, and what do you want us to do?"

He would reveal to us where to go, and what we should do. On this occasion, the Lord directed us to go to Illinois to a minister friend that we had not seen or heard from for years. In times past, we ministered back and forth to each other. When we needed help, they would show up in our driveway and tell us that God told them to come, that we needed help.

The same with us, God would let us know that they needed help, and would send us to them. We shared this ministry with several minister friends as well.

I do hope you have this kind of relationship with God and with your close minister friends. We saw each other through some very hard spiritual battles, and many difficult times. This was one of those times. The Lord showed us that this family was hurting and needed help and that we should go to them.

NOTE: Please do not shut yourself off when you are struggling, or hurting, and can't seem to get through your problems, situations, battles or your spiritual warfare. We need each other for there is strength among the family of God. Allow someone to minister to you.

It would be wise to build relationships like I have shared, with close minister friends. Comfort each other, pray together, strengthen one another, and stand together. There is strength in numbers. Hold each other's hands up as Aaron and Hur did for Moses. As long as your hands are heavenward, you are winning your battle.

PLEASE, DON'T LET THE DEVIL WIN!!!

You are a member of the FAMILY OF GOD.
Families never quit on each other!
Don't quit on yourself!
Don't quit on God!

He has done so much for you. He promised that He would <u>NEVER LEAVE OR FORSAKE YOU</u>!

He has also given His angels charge over you to keep you in all your ways. Never forget this!

Please read Psalms Chapter 91, Matt4:6, Luke 4:10-11,

So, we obeyed the prompting of the Holy Spirit, and headed for Illinois and our minister friends.

When we entered the town where our friend pastored, we stopped at a restaurant to eat. The owner came over to our table and asked if we were God's Children. We replied that we were. She told us that she knew it the minute we walked in.

She related how she had been a child of God, that she had allowed her restaurant business to come between her and Jesus and now she was miserable because she had lost out with Him.

We witnessed to her, and assured her that we would be praying for her to get her heart right with Jesus. We felt God not only sent us to this city for our friends, but for her as well.

We left there and went to visit our friends. When we drove into the driveway of our friends, they came out to see who was there. When they saw us, they said,

"What are you doing here?"

We replied,

"God told us you needed us, so here we are."

It did not take long to understand why God sent us there. We visited for a while, and our friend asked us to preach a revival, and we agreed.

Night after night, the services, the pastor, his family, and the congregation was bound spiritually. We spent day and night in the church seeking God to break the chains that were destroying the church, this pastor and his family.

When the breakthrough came, the Glory of the Lord filled that place, the altars were filled. The Pastor, his family, and congregation repented. Old feelings passed away, and all things became new. Joy filled the hearts and lives of that pastor, his family, and congregation as they rededicated their lives to God.

NOTE: *Only Jesus can make this kind of difference, and satisfy the soul of mankind. God accomplished His Plan and His Will in that place. To God, all the glory, honor and praise for what He had done.*

As we were leaving that town, we returned to the little restaurant. There was something different about the atmosphere, and especially the owner. She had a glow about her. She told us that God sent us to wake her up. After we left, she went into the back room, and got right with God. Her staff had accepted Jesus as well. It was awesome.

The restaurant was full of people, and she was speaking loud enough that everyone could hear how God had changed her life. When God comes on the scene, He makes a difference in the lives of those who hear His Voice, and obey. No telling how many lives were transformed by the power of the Living Jesus that day.

God still leads His dear children along. As a "Preacher, a Preacher's Wife, a Woman in Ministry", you too are led by the Holy Spirit. It is His plan that wherever we go, the Holy Spirit goes before us, and prepares the way for us to touch the lives of all we come in contact with.

He leads us by still waters, to restore our soul.
He leads us by His Spirit, and empowers us to overcome.
He sustains us, and covers us with His Blood.
He promises that He will never leave or forsake us.

When we are sensitive to His Voice, and determined to follow where He leads us, we will be amazed at the opportunities to minister to hungry souls.

GOD CLOSES SOME DOORS BEFORE US, AND OPENS OTHER DOORS TO US

God always has a purpose in everything He does. When He closes a door before us, we must trust Him, so we can be sensitive to His plan for our lives and our ministries and to walk through that new door opened to us.

WHY DOES GOD CLOSE DOORS BEFORE US?

He did not open the door.
We have tried to open a way of escape from a situation.
We are trying to run from Him.
He is trying to get our attention.
He sees danger or problems ahead.
He sees we are staggering in our commitment.
He knows Satan is setting a trap before us.
He knows Satan is trying to distract us from God's Plan for us.
He shuts doors to shelter and protect us.
He shuts doors to get us alone with Him.
And many more reasons.

GOD ALSO OPENS OTHER DOORS TO US.

He Goes before us and prepares the way.
He opens a door to us, and no man can shut it.
He gives direction for our life and ministry.
He opens doors of blessing.
He says, "I am the door to your future."
Acts 14:27, He opens the door to our faith.
John 10: 7, 9, He says, "I am the door of the sheepfold."
2 Cor. 2:12, He opens doors of ministries.
Col. 4:3, He opens a door of anointing to pray and to minister.

Revelation 3:8, *"I know thy works: behold, I have set before thee an open door, and no man can shut it: for thou hast a little strength, and hast kept My Word, and hast not denied My Name."*

THE BATTLE IS THE LORD'S

I had not shared my situation with anyone. God alone knew what I was struggling with.

I attended a revival meeting in another community. The evangelist did not know me and had no knowledge of my situation. During the service he stopped his message and pointed right at me and said,

"I have a word from God for you. Yes you, the lady in the blue dress. Will you please come forward?"

Now, I am a little hesitant to take a word from God from someone else. It concerns me when God doesn't speak to me and tell me what He wants me to know. However, since the evangelist insisted that I come forward I thought perhaps, God did have a word for me, so I obeyed. The evangelist came down from the pulpit and faced me. He told me that He had a word from God for me. He said,

"This is God's Word for you: He knows that you have a heart to do a work for Him. And, He knows that doors have been closed before you. He will open doors to you that no one can shut. He will go before you and prepare your way. He will stop the mouths of lions, and bring those into your life to bless you. This is God's promise to you from this time forward."

He prayed for me, went back to the pulpit and continued his message. I accepted this word because he described exactly what I was going through, so I knew this was a word of confirmation from God for me.

This was another time when God used one of His children to confirm an answer to my prayer.

NOTE: *After this, amazing doors were opened to me. No more doors closed before me.*

The next time the person who always made derogatory remarks to me and about me started their usual put down it came forth as blessings, compliments, and encouragement. The expression on their face changed as if to say, "THAT IS NOT WHAT I INTENDED TO SAY!"

From that time forward, every time this person spoke to or about me, it was indeed blessing.

When that took place and God changed the heart, and brought forth blessings, it was all I could do to contain myself because: I knew it was the Holy Spirit at work. Inside, I was standing up and shouting, *"THANK YOU JESUS!"* However, on the outside, the Holy Spirit helped me to remain calm, and respectful.

NOTE: *Now isn't that just like our Jesus, to fight our battles and to cause those who would wound, hurt or try to destroy us, would no longer be able to do so, but could only speak blessings to us, and over us.*

There may be times when you are dealing with those who seem to enjoy bringing hurt to you, to your husband, or your family. Commit them to God for Him to deal with. Jesus does not want us to fight our own battles especially those battles that come because of your commitment to the ministry. He tells us that: "The Battle is the Lords". The Bible says in:

> **Exodus 14:14, "The Lord shall fight for you, and ye shall hold your peace."**

2 Chronicles 20:15, 17, "......Thus saith the Lord unto you, "Be not afraid or dismayed by reason of this great multitude; for the battle is not yours, but God's."

V17, "Ye shall not need to fight in this battle: set yourselves, stand ye still, and see the salvation of the Lord with you, O Judah and Jerusalem: fear not, nor be dismayed; tomorrow go out against them: for the Lord will be with you."

2 Chronicles 32:7-8, "Be strong and courageous, be not afraid nor dismayed for the king of Assyria, nor for all the multitude that is with him: <u>for there be more with us than with him:"</u>

V8, "With him is an arm of flesh; but with us is the Lord our God to help us, and to fight our battles, <u>and the people rested themselves upon the words of Hezekiah</u> king of Judah."

NOTE: *Some have battled in their own strength, trying to face problems in their own power. They get wounded, and suffer hurtful scars. Some have even left the ministry because of those hurtful scars. Please do not allow that to happen to you, your husband, or your family. Remember, the battle is the Lords. He will fight for you, because,* **HE DOES NOT WANT YOU TO HAVE BATTLE SCARS.**

This is why the Bible instructs us to be filled with the Holy Spirit, which gives us power to overcome, to stand firm, and ward off the fiery darts of Satan and those who would hurt or destroy us.

NOTE: *Place your complete confidence and trust in Jesus, give it all to Him! Then stand back and watch the Holy Spirit open doors that no man can shut, close mouths and change hearts.*

SOMETIMES GOD DELAYS OR INTERRUPTS OUR PLANS

Plans had been made for my first Missions trip out of the country. I was on my way to be with one of our Missionary families who had gone through terrifying situations, when war broke out in their country. My flight was interrupted and I was stranded alone in a foreign country.

I complained because I felt I needed to be with them and now I was delayed in a place where I did not know anyone, I did not speak or understand the language, and I definitely did not want to be there! I sat beside a window looking out, thinking,

"Why am I here Lord, and why is my schedule delayed?"

The presence of the Lord flooded that place. He told me He had interrupted my schedule because He wanted this time alone with me. All night, He poured into my spirit.

He knew I needed to be prepared for what was ahead. He gave me a peace and assurance that He was preparing the way before me, and when ministry opportunities were given, He would be there with a fresh anointing for each situation.

What a precious time when I finally arrived at my destination, God blessed, and many lives were touched and changed. I am so sorry I complained so much. I am learning to be content in whatsoever state I find myself.

To God I give all glory, honor and praise. I am so glad, He interrupted my plans and we spent precious time together. Jeremiah says it well...

> *Jeremiah 29: 11-14, "For I know the thoughts that I think toward you," saith the Lord, " thoughts of peace, and not of evil, to give you an expected end."*

V12, "Then shall ye call upon Me, and ye shall go and pray unto Me, and I will hearken unto you."

V13, "And ye shall seek Me, and find Me, when ye shall search for Me with all your heart."

V14, "And I will be found of you," saith the Lord."

AND, I SAY,

"THANK YOU LORD,

FOR ALL YOUR PROMISES

FOR LEADING ME DAY BY DAY AND

FOR INTERUPTING MY SCHEDULE AND MY PLANS"

Chapter 4

NEVER A DULL MOMENT IN THE PARSONAGE

THOSE GOOD OLD DAYS

In days of old, the church owned the house the preacher's family lived in. The ladies of the church decorated it to their taste, and came regularly to inspect it.

Now if, the preacher's wife had moved a chair, or changed a picture on the wall, they let her know that this was their parsonage, and they had decorated it just the way they wanted it to be, and she was not to move anything: period!

I hope those good old days are in the past. In today's world, you may own your own home. We will refer to it as the parsonage.

(A parsonage is where the preacher's family lives whether it belongs to the church, or it is owned by the preacher).

THAT FAMILY IN THE PARSONAGE

The preacher's family is supposed to be perfect! That is according to most congregations.

However, in reality, the preacher's family is just like most families in the church. They have their ups, and downs. There are days of perfect harmony, and days when everyone gets on everybody's last nerve. Oh, those good old days.

PASTOR AND PASTOR'S WIFE, OR HUSBAND AND WIFE

As a young Pastor's Wife, I often wondered: who pastors the Pastor's Wife? There were times when I needed a pastor, and times when I needed my husband, not a pastor. Where is the dividing line? How does one separate the two?

There must be a clear cut difference if the marriage is to be successful and the ministry fulfilled. Guidelines must be established.

TWO HATS AND A HATRACK

I may have found an answer: I recall an interview with a husband and wife that took place many years ago. Both were actors and worked together every day. The question was asked,

"How do you manage your career and your marriage since you work together and live together all the time day after day?"

This was the couple's response. They said,

"Our lives are like that old TV program, "*I LED THREE LIVES*". In that program, the person led three totally different lives, and kept each of them separated and a secret, so that those involved in each life, did not know anything about the other two lives."

"We live two lives. In one life we are both actors working together all day long, every day.

In the other life, we are husband and wife living together at home. We have developed this ritual which has been and is the secret of our happiness."

"Each of us has two hats. We have a hat rack at our door. When leaving the house for our jobs, we stop at the hat rack, and put on our actor hats, go out and take on our career. When we come home at night, we stop at the hat rack, take off our actor hats and put on our husband and wife hats and enjoy our time together."

"Our lives change at the hat rack. The two lives are kept separate that way. When we change hats, we leave that life at the hat rack, keeping the stresses of each life to itself."

NOTE: *People in the congregation may have set a good example for the parsonage family. They probably have a job with hours from nine to five. When they punch the time card at five o'clock they leave their days work at the office. When they get home, they enjoy the evening with their family.*

What happens at the office stays at the office! What happens at home stays at home! They are able to keep a good balance between their work, and their family. I sometimes wonder, if they have two hats and a hat rack at their front door!

THE TWO LIVES OF THE PASTOR AND THE PASTOR'S WIFE

LIFE 1... A husband and his wife and their children at home
LIFE 2...The preacher and the preacher's wife at church

What would happen if the pastor and pastor's wife had two hats each and a hat rack at the front door? When we take on the roll of pastor and pastor's wife: we would put on our ministry hats and proceed to pastoral care of the congregation.

This includes: conducting services; prayer time and sermon preparation; praying for each family; visiting the sick and shut-ins; counseling when needed; taking care of church business and solving problems, the list goes on and on.

When we came home, we would take off our ministry hats hang them on the hat rack at the door leaving the ministry life, its needs and problems at the hat rack.

We exchange our ministry hats, for our husband and wife hats at the hat rack and start our second life. We take on the life of just husband and wife enjoying activities and private family time together, just like the families of the church enjoys their private family time and activities when they leave their jobs.

We dearly love both of our lives and this would help us keep each one in proper perspective. The congregation may call the pastor if there is an emergency or urgent need. We will go to the hat rack, change into our ministry hats, and respond. This helps to keep a good balance for both lives.

Once in our house, it becomes our sanctuary. We leave the cares and problems of our ministry life at the hat rack, and retreat to our family life just being a husband to his wife, and a wife to her husband, and Mom and Dad to the children.

This way we are successful in both of our lives, and grow closer to each other in our roles as husband and wife, Mom and Dad to the kids and preacher and preacher's wife to the church.

Keeping peace in the parsonage: Brother Pastor and Sister Pastor's Wife it is up to you. Each must keep your own vineyard so to speak. You really do live two lives, yet those lives are intertwined: one in the ministry and one in the parsonage.

Perhaps, you should purchase a hat rack, a preacher and a preacher's wife hat, and a husband and a wife hat, and place them at the door of the parsonage! The Apostle Paul said in:

1 Corinthians 9:23-27; V 27, "But I keep under my body, and bring it into subjection: lest that by any means, when I have preached to others, I myself should be a castaway."

LIVING IN A GOLDFISH BOWL

Sister Pastor's Wife, have you ever felt like you were living in a goldfish bowl? Ever pastored in a community where *everyone* knows *everything* about *everybody*?

At this church we pastored, the parking lot was between the church and the parsonage. Some cars parked facing the parsonage. Can you visualize what it would be like to live in a goldfish bowl? Picture this:

LOOK EVERYBODY, THERE'S A CAR IN THE PREACHER'S BEDROOM

One Sunday evening, a man was parking his car facing the parsonage. Unable to stop in time, he drove his car through our bedroom wall. He was not injured but was pretty shook up. It was a sight to behold, a car in the preacher's bedroom.

When his car was moved, there was a giant gaping hole that revealed everything in our bedroom. Of course word spread quickly about the hole in the parsonage wall. People were curious, and seemed anxious to see the sight.

It was like living in a goldfish bowl with the people peering in pointing at what they saw.

Life is never dull when living in a church parsonage goldfish bowl.

DRIVE BY'S: JUST TO SEE IF THE PREACHER'S WIFE HAS ANYTHING NEW

While at this church, I had a washer, but no clothes dryer. So, it was necessary to hang clothes on the clothes line outside. People would drive slowly by the parsonage when they saw clothes hanging on the line, so they could see if the "Preacher's Wife" had anything new.

If, I hung anything new on the line, some of the ladies would let me know that they noticed that I had a lot of new clothes hanging on the clothes line. We must be doing pretty well if we could afford all those new clothes.

In those days I made nearly all of our clothes. I could purchase material for four or five dollars and make outfits for myself and for Debbie too.

This went on the entire time we pastored that church. Every time we got anything new, the whole town knew about it. They knew if we were at home, and every time we had company. It made me feel like I was living in a goldfish bowl.

I told my preacher husband, that I hoped the next church we pastored, would be six miles out of town. Then I could hang out clothes and nobody would notice if we had anything new, if we had company, or if we wanted to chase each other around the house, nobody would be watching every move we made.

NOTE: *You MUST be careful what you say, Sister Pastor's wife! God is always listening to our wishes. Would you believe? When God led us from that church to our next pastorate, it was indeed, "six miles out of town".*

Now, I had a clothes dryer and no one could tell if we had anything new. If they wanted to know if we were gone, or if we had company, they had to drive six miles out of town. Best of all, I no longer felt like I was living in a Goldfish Bowl.

PREACHER, DON'T GET A NEW CAR!

When we quit our jobs and moved to another state to accept the pastorate of a small rural church. We were driving an old worn out 1953 Chevrolet. The transmission was bad, and reverse gear did not work most of the time.

Word came to us that if we got a new car, the people would be very unhappy with us. The congregation had the mindset that when former pastors bought a new car soon after they came to the church, that they were just after the people's money and that he just came there to get rich.

Several pastors had left the church, shortly after they got their new car. In fact, this church had gone through seven pastors in ten years.

We prayed for wisdom, because we really needed a better more dependable car but remembering what we had been told, we kept driving the old "53 Chevy".

Our little church had great people in it. They were faithful to go to fellowship meetings and youth rallies. We could always count on taking a car load with us. On this occasion, we had taken a deacon and his wife to a fellowship meeting which was about forty miles from home.

On the return trip, the spring broke that controlled the accelerator. The old Chevy would only go as fast as it was idling. So there we were, putt, putt, putting along all the way home. People kept passing us, rolling down their windows asking if we needed help. Bill just waved them on, and said,

"I think we can make it. Thanks anyway."

It was quite late when we finally got back to our little town. We took the deacon and his wife home and headed for the parsonage.

The next day, the phone rang most of the day. People began calling the parsonage saying,

"Pastor we are praying for you to get a new car. The deacon and his wife told us that they were afraid that they would never get home last night because the pastor's car would hardly go. So, Please Pastor, try to get a better car as soon as possible!"

NOTE: *Well now, God really does work in mysterious ways! Imagine this: He let a little spring break when He had the right people in our old Chevy. He changed the mindset of a whole congregation just because of a little broken accelerator spring!*

GOD REALLY DOES HAVE A SENSE OF HUMOR! Isn't our God amazing? It pays to seek God in every situation. He will work His plan when we wait patiently on Him even if He allows a little spring to break on the accelerator of an old 1953 Chevy.

THERE'S A STRANGE MAN SITTING ON MY BED!

There was never a dull moment living in the parsonage. Sometimes it gets down right exciting. I never knew what would happen next. What a life, being a preacher's wife.

I woke up one morning and when I opened my eyes, I saw that there was a strange man sitting on the foot of my bed looking at me. I yelled for my husband,

"BILLLLLL!" "WHO IS THIS STRANGE MAN? WHY IS HE IN OUR BEDROOM AND, WHY IS HE SITTING ON FOOT OF OUR BED LOOKING AT ME?"

As Bill ushered the man out of our bedroom, the man said,

"I just wanted to meet the new preacher and his wife. I want you to come to our house tonight for supper. You will come won't you?"

Bill agreed to his request and showed him out the door.

Now, this older gentleman loved to talk, and did so nonstop. He also liked to hug the ladies.

We were invited to their house fairly often. One day at their house, I was washing dishes. He kept trying to hug me. I told him that if he didn't stop, I would wash his face with my greasy dish rag.

Knowing he would return, I scooped up greasy residue on the dish rag. The next time he tried to hug me I smeared his face with that greasy rag. He jumped back, and said,

"You are the preacher's wife I thought you were too nice to do anything like that."

I told him, that from that point on, I would only shake hands with him because, the only men I allow to hug me, was my husband and my daddy.

NOTE: *He told everyone in town, what that preacher's wife did to him and, if they met her they should only shake hands with her and, not try to hug her because: she would wash their face with a greasy dish rag because, she didn't let any man hug her but her husband and her daddy. After that, I got lots of handshakes!*

LEARNING TO GUARD MY WORDS

We usually rested Sunday afternoon so we would be fresh for the evening service. This man and his wife would come to the parsonage on Sunday afternoon expecting to eat. On this occasion I used paper plates. He volunteered to throw them away. I told him that we are just poor preachers and we had to wash them and use them at least three times. He took me seriously and proceeded to wash out the paper plates.

On another Sunday afternoon, their car stopped in front of the parsonage. I was a little frustrated and said,

"Oh no, here he comes, it will be talk, talk, talk."

Well, I was not aware that his sweet wife had already come into the house. She heard what I said, and was deeply hurt. I felt terrible that I had not engaged brain before opening my mouth. I apologized to her, for what I had said, and she was kind enough to forgive me.

I learned a valuable lesson that day that words once spoken can never be taken back. They can either bless, or they can wound. The Bible tells us in,

> **Psalms 19:14, "Let the words of my mouth, and the meditation of my heart, be acceptable in thy sight, O Lord, my Strength and my Redeemer."**

> **Proverbs 15:1-2, "A soft answer turneth away wrath: but grievous words stir up anger."**

> **V2, "The tongue of the wise useth knowledge aright: but the mouth of fools poureth out foolishness."**

NOTE: *As a child of God, and especially since we are women in ministry and leadership, we must use words wisely. I learned to keep my words sweet, because I may have to eat them later! Our attitude, and what we say, reflects our relationship with the Lord, and will affect our influence on those we minister too, for the cause of Christ.*

FRUSTRATION AND GOLF BALLS

Have you ever been totally frustrated with someone in the congregation?

Everything is going great, and first thing you knew there was trouble brewing, or someone was stirring up problems and getting on your last nerve. It happens to the best of us.

Exodus Chapter 32, records how God and Moses were frustrated with the Children of Israel. **Verse 7,** God gives the Children of Israel to Moses because,

> *Exodus 32: 7, "And the Lord said unto Moses, "Go, get thee down; <u>for thy people which thou broughtest out of the land of Egypt,</u> have corrupted themselves."*

Later **in Verse 11,** Moses gives those same people back to God,

> *V 11, "And Moses besought the Lord his God, and said, "Lord, why doth Thy wrath wax hot against <u>THY PEOPLE, which Thou hast brought forth out of the land of Egypt with great power, and with a mighty hand?"</u>*

NOTE: *How amusing, at times neither wanted to claim them. This makes us know that we will encounter times when all is not well in the house of God. So how do we deal with our frustration?*

My preacher husband had his own special way of dealing with his frustration. He never went off anyone in the church, nor did he use the pulpit to vent his frustration.

My preacher husband had a set of golf clubs he kept in the closet. When he was totally frustrated, or when someone got on his very last nerve, he would simply take his golf clubs out of the closet, pick up a bucket of golf balls and a pen and go out behind the church.

Now, the church and parsonage was up on a hill. Behind the church there was a deep gully and a heavily wooded area.

He would take a golf ball out of his bucket, write the name of the person who had frustrated him on it and set it on the tee.

Then, he would quietly call their name, and hit that golf ball out into space, down the hill and into the woods. I knew how frustrated he was, by how long he stayed, and how many golf balls he used.

When he was finished, he picked up his golf clubs and bucket, and calmly returned to the parsonage and placed them back in the closet. Then he sat down on the couch with a big smile on his face, perfectly at ease, frustration gone with the golf balls.

NOTE: I often wondered, what if, someone would go down into those woods and find all those golf balls laying around on the ground with the names of church members on them. Can you imagine the thoughts that would run through their mind?

I wonder: how do you and your preacher husband deal with your frustrations?

WHO'S BEEN JUMPING ON MY BED?

When we became pastors of this church, we went into a new building which was not yet completed. The bathrooms had not been installed.

The congregation used the bathroom in the parsonage.

I would come home after church, and find my bed messed up and dirty shoe prints all over my white bedspread and pillows strewn all around. It was well made, neat and clean when I left for church. So I started taking notice of who was leaving the church during the service.

I noticed that several sweet little church kids slipped out of the service, one at a time, to go to the bathroom. When they didn't return, I went to investigate. When I entered the parsonage, it sounded like a wild party was taking place.

I went immediately to investigate. When I entered the bedroom, I found the reason they had not returned to the service. They were jumping up and down and running around on my bed, leaving their dirty shoe prints on my white bedspread. To top it all off, they were using all my pillows in a pillow fight.

When they saw me, they jumped down off the bed, and started for the door. I blocked their exit. I lined them up and we went back to the church, and I sat them down beside me. When service was over, their parents wanted to know if there was a problem!

I invited them to the parsonage to check out *"the problem".* I asked the kids to explain to their parents what they had been doing. The parents insisted that they apologize for their actions, and stated that they would accompany their child to the parsonage bathroom if they needed to leave the service.

I thanked the parents, and accepted the apologies of the sweet little church kids and there were no more pillow fights at the parsonage during church. There are ways to handle those little things that could really irritate you so they don't become a major problem or upset.

THE BRAND NEW BRAIDED RUG

I had saved for a long time to purchase this room size braided rug. Our policy was to save for what we wanted or needed, until we could purchase it, this way we did not incur any debt.

When we had revivals the evangelists stayed in the parsonage with us. During one revival, the evangelist's little boy wanted to polish his shoes. He accidently spilled the whole bottle of black liquid shoe polish on my new braided rug.

How would you react in this situation?

You could become angry and make remarks that would destroy a beautiful friendship and inflict wounds that might last a lifetime.

Or, you can choose to remain calm, cool and collected and assure that accidents do happen and all is forgiven. Clean the rug, and have a great day and a mighty outpouring of the Holy Spirit in the revival.

After that, when anything was spilled, the comment would be: *"That's what the rug is for: to soak up spills."*

MOOCH AND THE SILVER CAR

Sunday morning, after church, everyone headed to the parking lot and home. Now, it had rained all week, and the old red clay had seeped through the gravel on the church parking lot.

A church member had a shiny silver town car that was his pride and joy so to speak. When he saw his car, he got very upset. There were tiny red clay paw prints all over his shiny car.

Sitting on the trunk was this large, long haired calico Persian cat. She had walked all over his car with her muddy feet. He quickly shooed that cat off his car and wanted to know whose cat this was.

It was Mooch, the preacher's cat. We apologized and offered to have his car washed, which he declined. He wanted us to know that he expected us to keep our cat off of his car.

Now Mooch the cat, had a mind of her own. If she could get out of the house when we had church, she would be waiting for this man, sitting on the trunk of his shinny silver car. She did not get on any other car on the parking lot, not even on ours.

The man would get so angry when he saw Mooch sitting on his shiny car.

From the altar of blessing, to the church parking lot, Satan would steal his victory before he even got home. Satan will point out situations that are insignificant, like he used the cat, who sat on the trunk of a car. He will make sure you see every little distraction he sets before your eyes.

NOTE: *It is Satan's plan to side track us. He does not care how much of a blessing you receive in church if he can steal it before you even get home. He will cause you to see little things as major problems and even to get blown out of proportion. We must be on our guard, and not allow anger and bitterness to creep in and take control of us and steal our peace and joy.*

Jesus gives us instructions to help us avoid allowing those distractions to side track us.

> *Matthew 10:16, "Behold, I send you forth as sheep in the midst of wolves: be ye therefore wise as serpents, and harmless as doves."*

1 Peter 5:8, "Be sober, be vigilant; because your adversary the devil, as a roaring lion, walketh about, seeking whom he may devour:"

Be wise to the sly tricks and traps of Satan. Guard your joy and your peace, so he cannot hinder your experience and relationship with God and with one another.

STOLEN CHICKENS IN THE PREACHER'S DEEP FREEZER

Like I said, there is never a dull moment in the Parsonage. The town drunk started coming to our church. Late one Saturday night, he knocked on our door. When the preacher answered it, the man handed him a gunny sack with ten very skinny live chickens in it. He said,

"Here preacher, I brought you these chickens because, you have been so good to me."

Bill asked him if they were his chickens, he assured Bill that they were. Bill thanked him for his gift, and took him home.

Now, Early Monday morning, we were leaving to take our youth to camp and would be gone for a week. We discussed what we were going to do about those poor skinny chickens since we would be gone for a week to camp.

We decided that, after church Sunday night, Bill would take them way out behind the church and prepared them for the freezer.

While he was out back, one of our neighbors called and told me that there was a strange man out behind the church, and that he was setting down doing something. She imagined that the man was drunk.

She indicated that she was going to call the police. I quickly assured her I would take care of it. *(I didn't tell her that it was only the preacher, dressing out those poor skinny chickens.)*

Days later, a man knocked on our door, when I answered it he said,

"I think the preacher has my chickens."

He stated that the chickens had been stolen and he was told that they had been given to the preacher. I invited him in so I could give him his ten skinny chickens from our freezer.

Previously, we had purchased a dozen large hens, and they were in our freezer as well. When the man saw the big fat hens, he said,

"Those are my chickens, I would recognize them anywhere."

I assured him that those <u>were not</u> his chickens.

I promptly took out his skinny chickens and gave them to him. He was not overly happy, but accepted them and went his way.

I thought, what if, word got out that the preacher had stolen chickens in his deep freeze. Can you imagine the talk of the town, if the front page of the news paper would have the preacher's picture on it with the caption, "Stolen Chickens were found in the Preacher's deep freezer".

Ahhhh, life in the parsonage sometimes it gets downright exciting!

Through the years, many wonderful experiences took place in the parsonage. Some I have shared here, others when God brought miracles and blessings are shared throughout the chapters of this book.

DEVIL DON'T YOU CROSS THAT LINE

A prison inmate spent most of his time in solitary confinement. There he found a Gideon Bible and began reading it. The Holy Spirit convicted him of his sin and he accepted Jesus as Savior. He prayed that God would get him out of prison and promised to serve Him the rest of his life.

God answered his prayer. One day, the warden told him to get his things together because he was getting out of prison that day! Before he knew it, he was standing outside the gates of that prison. This was indeed a miracle.

This man, his wife and six little children were in our church. Another family in the church mentored this family watching over them every day. In spite of their efforts, the man began drinking, and got back on drugs.

On this occasion, he was beating his family. Bill as pastor, was called to intervene.

We managed to get his family out of the house and brought them to the parsonage where they would be safe. The man was so high on drugs that he was like a wild man with super human strength. He came to the parsonage looking for his family. He broke the antenna off of our car, and tied it in a knot.

He started for the front door ranting and raving trying to get to his family. He was making violent threats, shouting out what he was going to do to us. He came on the porch and intended to come into the house, still threatening our lives.

There was not time to call a prayer meeting. Only time to say,

"JESUS, HELP US!"

When you call His name, you have His full attention. *The anointing of the Holy Spirit took control. It was the Holy Spirit that spoke through me that night.*

I looked straight into the man's eyes, and with my finger, I drew an imaginary line across the threshold of the parsonage doorway. I said,

"IN THE NAME OF JESUS, I TAKE AUTHORITY OVER YOU! DEVIL, YOU CROSS THAT LINE AND YOU ARE DEAD!"

He backed off and kept backing all the way out to the street. He kept making threats, but could not come on the porch again. It took six police officers to get him into the police car and take him to jail.

When he got out of jail, he came to the parsonage. We invited him in, and the three of us sat down at the dining room table. He apologized and questioned how we could welcome him into our home, after what he had done. We told him that we loved him and Jesus loved him too.

He asked Jesus to forgive him that morning, and to help him be the kind of man, husband and father that God wanted him to be.

And of course, Jesus forgave him, took him back, and so did we. He said,

"Preacher, I can't do much of anything good. But if you will put your shoes out on the front step every night, I will polish them for you every day, and bring them back early every morning." He kept his word, and made sure the preacher's shoes were polished and shined every day.

THE HOLY SPIRIT IN THE LIFE OF THE BELIEVER

The Holy Spirit dwells *within us* and gives us anointing, wisdom, and power to overcome whatever Satan throws into our path. Most of all,

Jesus has given you and me authority to use His Name. There is no other name like the Name of Jesus. There is power in His Name.

> *Luke 10:19, "Behold, I give unto you power to tread on serpents and scorpions, and over all the power of the enemy: and nothing shall by any means hurt you."*

This does not mean for you to go out and step on a snake, or pick up scorpions. It means that He has given you power and anointing to overcome them. Just as Paul when the deadly viper fastened on his hand, and he shook it off into the fire.

NOTE: When you face satanic powers, the Holy Spirit gives you power and authority to deal with them, and to overcome them, as He did for me when I faced this threat to our lives. The Bible says in,

> *John 14:12-18, "Verily, verily, I say unto you, he that believeth on Me, the works that I do shall he do also; and greater works than these shall he do: because I go to My Father."*

> *V13, "And <u>whatsoever ye shall ask in My Name,</u> that will I do, that the Father may be glorified in the Son."*

> *V14, <u>"If ye shall ask anything in My Name, I will do it."</u>*

> *V15, "If ye love Me, keep My Commandments."*

> *V16, "And I will pray the Father, and He shall give you another Comforter, that He may abide with you forever."*

> *V17, "Even the Spirit of Truth, Whom the world cannot receive, because it seeth Him not, neither knoweth Him; <u>but ye know Him; for He dwelleth with you, and shall be in you."</u>*

V18, "I will not leave you comfortless: I will come to you."

You choose how you react to each situation you face. It is up to you to decide how you allow it to affect your life, your family and your ministry.

Be instant in season and out of season, means, that your life is saturated with the Holy Spirit *"continually"* so when the occasion arises, you can be like Sampson in the Bible.

When the Holy Spirit would come upon him, with strength, nothing or no one could overcome or defeat him. It was only when he let down his spiritual guard, that he was defeated.

In Sampson's day, the Holy Spirit came upon him, at times.

In our day, His Spirit <u>dwells in us</u>. When we receive the Baptism into the Holy Spirit, this gives us continual power and anointing equipping us to overcome any situation we face whatever comes our way.

What an exciting, privileged awesome life we live as, the Preacher's Wife and Women in the Ministry. Living life in the parsonage is exciting because, there is never a dull moment!

Chapter 5

RAISING AWESOME
PREACHER'S KIDS

EVERYBODY WATCHES THE PREACHER'S KIDS

All eyes are on the PK'S, (preacher's kids). Everything they do is scrutinized. They are no different from the deacon's kids, or any other church member's kids, they are kids. They do have advantages however, because they are being raised in the preacher's home.

They will likely experience all kinds of criticism and hear remarks made by disgruntled church people who make sure that "PKs" hear what they think of their parents. In spite of all that, they are fortunate to be the preacher's kids. They learn to deal with and to overcome what they see and hear by our example as we live our everyday life.

One can pair up the kids with their parents, by observing their actions and their attitudes, for our kids reflect whatever they have learned or heard from us as their parents.

In fact, you might say that they are a "little you"! Preacher's kids and church kids spend more time in the home with their parents then in the church. The home is where they develop their attitudes and their spiritual and moral values.

They learn how to take responsibility for their actions; how to cope with problems, and how to value what is important in their Christian life, from watching how their parents live and conduct their lives.

GOALS FOR RAISING OUR KIDS

The goal in raising awesome and godly church and preacher's kids is for them to love Jesus with all their heart, soul and spirit. To walk the walk, talk the talk and live the life that is pleasing to our heavenly Father.

When they are grown, they will go one of two ways. Either they will love God, the church and the ministry, or they will turn against God, the church and the ministry.

I have witnessed the families whose kids follow in their footsteps with the call of God on their lives.

Sad to say, I have witnessed those who have been hurt, they became bitter and turned their back on anything spiritual breaking the heart of God, and of their parents.

The preacher's kids are carefully watched by everyone to see if they are doing anything they should not be doing. Sometimes it is to confront the pastor or pastor's wife about their kids. Sometimes it is to justify the behavior of their own children.

GUILTY OR NOT GUILTY

When Debbie was about three years old, she sat on the front bench at church while her daddy and I were on the platform. We could watch and correct her by a finger snap, or eye contact making sure she was the good little preacher's kid.

People were amazed at the way she would sit there by herself until I came down from the platform after song service.

A man in the church always had candy for the little preacher's kid. She would stick her hand through the slats in the back of the bench and he would put candy in it. She knew not to eat it until she got home.

One night, a lady asked me if I knew Debbie was eating candy in church. I took the ladies word and disciplined Debbie without giving her a chance to tell me that she was not guilty.

Debbie opened her little hand and showed me the piece of candy still in the rapper. Can you imagine how terrible I felt when I found out I had punished her for something she did not do?

I picked her up sat her on my lap and hugged her. Then, I told her Mommy was so sorry for punishing her for something that she did not do. I told her that I was wrong and asked her to please forgive me.

I promised her that I would always give her opportunity to tell her side of the situation. I kept my word to her from that moment on through all her life.

IT IS OKAY TO SAY, "I'M SORRY" TO YOUR KIDS

Now, I know there are those who say you should not apologize to your children. That to admit to them that you were wrong is a sign of weakness as a parent.

Let me say here: How can we teach our children to admit that they were wrong, when they were wrong, and to say they are sorry and ask forgiveness if they never see their parents set the example before them?

This is one of the best ways, we can teach our children honesty and respect for themselves, and others, most of all, to take responsibility for their actions and not blame someone else.

BUILDING TRUST IN YOUR KIDS

A story goes that a dad gave his son the keys to the car, with instructions to: obey the law; not get careless; that driving was a privilege and a great responsibility. He told him that if he broke the law, or got a ticket, that he would have to give up the keys and his privilege to drive the car. The son replied,

"Well Dad, how will you know if I speed, break the law, get a ticket or drive carelessly and get in trouble?"

The Dad simply said,

"Son, I will know when you come to me and hand over the keys to the car."

If our children know that we trust and respect them, they will respect themselves and do their best to please us and will learn to take responsibility for their actions.

BECAUSE, YOU ARE "THE PREACHER'S KID"

When Debbie was growing up in the parsonage there were places we did not go, and things we did not participate in. We always taught her that we lived our life as best we knew how to be pleasing to God according to His Word, not to please people or a congregation.

We were careful to avoid situations, places and things that might hinder our walk with Jesus.

We did not teach or tell her: that she could or could not do something because the congregation would not like it. Or, that she had to be an example because she was "The Preacher's Kid."

We taught her to: love Jesus with all her heart, live her life to please Him. Most of all, when she pleased Jesus in her every day walk and talk, she would be happy with herself. She would not live with regrets, grief, heartache or shame.

She grew up with a love for the things of God, for the ministry and the church. She delighted in working and serving in the church and in the ministry.

SAVED AT THE AGE OF THREE

Debbie was three years old. She was kneeling beside me at a cottage prayer meeting. She began to cry, I heard her saying,

"Oh Jesus, Save me Jesus, I'm a bad old sinner Jesus, forgive me Jesus. Come into my heart. I love you Jesus, I want to be your child forever. I give you all of me. Please, save me Jesus so I can go to heaven."

When I looked at her, her eyes were closed and tears were running down her little cheeks. She was praying with all her heart. As I listened to her, my heart was so full, that at this young age, on her own, she accepted Jesus as Savior, and later received the baptism in the Holy Spirit.

What a testimony that she lived all her life for Jesus. That she had nothing in her past to bring her heartache and regret. She loved to preach to her little friends and pray with them to get saved.

When she was just a toddler, I became very ill. She came up to the bed and said,

"Mommy, you want me pray for you?"

I said,

"Yes honey, please pray for Mommy."

She laid hands on me and said,

"O Jesus, heal my Mommy. Amen!"

She ran off to continue playing. In a few minutes she came back to the bed and said,

"Get up Mommy I prayed for you,
Jesus healed you. Get up Mommy!"

I knew I had to make an effort to get up. Her faith and trust in God was at stake. When I got up, I was healed. I trust and value the prayers of a child as much as anyone I know. The child like faith and trust of a child is a gift from God.

As Spirit filled parents, we recognize that God is working His plan in the lives of our kids. We recognize the gifts God is bestowing on them, and carefully help them develop those gifts and talents.

Debbie was always a vital part of our ministry. She began playing a little twelve base accordion at church when she was about six years old. She loved to play and sing, most of all she loved praying with people around the altar.

Begin training and encouraging your children to participate in the ministry starting when they are very young so it becomes a vital part of their life, preparing them to fulfill God's plan for their future whatever it may be.

God's plan of Salvation is so simple even a little child can understand and respond when the Holy Spirit touches their hearts.

How precious it is when a child accepts Jesus as Savior and lives all their life guided by the Holy Spirit. They avoid pitfalls that could destroy them. When they are grown, they will not have the scars of sin in their past to deal with.

What a powerful testimony, that they were never delivered from drugs, cigarettes, alcohol, pornography, or sexual permissiveness, but have the testimony that they walked with God, all of their lives.

I love to see little children worshiping with eyes closed, and hands raised toward heaven, lost in the presence of God. Oh how important it is to nurture and encourage their worship and their progress in the things of God beginning when they are young and continue when they are grown.

> *Mark 10:13-16, "And they brought young children to Him, that He should touch them: and His disciples rebuked those that brought them."*
>
> *V14, "But when Jesus saw it, He was much displeased, and said unto them, "Suffer the little children to come unto Me, and forbid them not: for of such is the kingdom of God."*
>
> *V15, "Verily, I say unto you, whosoever shall not receive the kingdom of God as a little child, he shall not enter therein."*
>
> *V16, "And He took them up in His arms, put His hands upon them, and blessed them."*

Does this not speak of how important children are to the Master? Parents brought their children for Him to touch them. He put His hands on them and blessed them.

Is it any wonder that little children open their hearts to Him, and they have a special relationship with Him when they are very young?

Many of our missionaries, preachers and preacher's wives were saved as children, and received a call to ministry.

As parents, we can encourage or discourage our children spiritually.

I had ministered in a children's service. When the altar call was given, several children came for salvation. One young girl about eight years old, stood out to me.

When she got up from the altar, she had tears in her eyes and a glow about her countenance. I asked her what happened to her. She told me that Jesus had come into her heart, and she felt so good inside.

After the service, her mother and others were visiting. I placed my arm around this little girl and commented about her experience. Her mother spoke up and said,

"Oh she didn't know what she was doing she just went up there because the other kids went. She is too young and doesn't understand this stuff."

That child looked at her mother, tucked her head, and her countenance changed immediately, the glow went out of her face. My heart was broken for that child. I have often wondered about her and if she ever came to an altar again.

"I PROMISE, WE WILL NOT LOSE HER!"

A parent in our church stood weeping asking for special prayer for her teenage son "J".

When service was over, Bill and I were at the altar interceding for "J". The Lord said to me,

"STOP PRAYING! Look around, where are "J's" parents, and where is their burden for their son?"

Then He told me to look at the front seat and tell Him what I saw. I told Him that I saw my child patiently waiting for me to finish praying. He said,

"Yes your child that you prayed for and I gave to you when doctors said you could not have a child."

Then He said,

"SHE IS YOUR PRIORITY!" I require her spiritual welfare and training at your hand. Go to her! Pick her up and love her! Teach her My Word and My ways. You dedicated her back to Me when I gave her to you. If you do your part to teach her, I will do My part to guide her and I promise, We will not lose her."

"I will require "J's" spiritual welfare and training at the hands of his parents."

The words: **"SHE IS YOUR PRIORITY! I require her spiritual welfare and training at your hand"** has been a constant reminder of my responsibility and privilege as her parent.

How precious is our opportunity to shape and mold the lives of those little ones that God has placed in our care!

As parents, WE WILL give account before God for the way we bring up and teach our children.

He has given us special insight and wisdom to help us establish godly principals and moral values into their lives.

We have the awesome charge to teach them that:

>   God loves them unconditionally
>   How to trust and accept His salvation and guidance
>   How to listen and obey Him
>   How to pray and receive answers to prayers
>   How to develop a consistent prayer life
>   How to read and study His Holy Word
>   How to apply His Word to their everyday life
>   How to take responsibility for their decisions

We teach by our example more than by our words. They observe our prayer life, our Bible reading and study, our trust and faith in God, our everyday <u>consistent</u> walk with Jesus.

DEALING WITH THE LOSS OF A PARENT

Debbie was only fifteen years old when her Daddy was called to his heavenly home. She asked me this question:

"Mom, do you know what this means?"

I asked her what it meant to her. She replied,

"Well, Since Daddy has gone to heaven, it means that you and I have a lot more to do now because we have to do what Daddy would have done if he was still here with us."

She was so strong and brave during those first days. We prayed together many times and comforted each other. Yet through it all, she locked away her grief until years later when she was in college.

She was a Daddy's girl, when she saw other dads coming to be with their kids, it took its toll on her emotions. All those feelings of grief and loss that she had locked away came in like a flood and overtook her.

The three of us had been very close. Now, the two of us were closer than ever. We prayed together and we cried together many times. God reminded me of His promise he had given to me so many years before.

He promised that, If, I did my part to raise and train her, He would do His part to guide and direct her. Now, I should place her in His loving care, and He again promised that: We would not lose her.

I have shared several incidents about Debbie, how she was brought up, and how God directed her life through those years.

NOTE: *It was hard to see her struggling with the loss of her Daddy. The Lord showed me that He had been with her through each phase of her life. How He was preparing and teaching her to lean on and trust Him in every situation she would encounter in her ever day life, and in her future.*

I realized that God could minister to her in ways far beyond my abilities. He brought her through this dark time in her life, and helped her deal with her grief. He continued to equip her to fulfill her potential, and to prepare her for what He had called her to be and to do.

I am so thankful for her dedication to the Lord, and to the ministry God had given to her. Even through the three years she battled cancer, she never once complained of her lot.

My prayer is, that other children who have lost a parent or a close loved one, can take comfort in knowing that God will guide them and will never leave them or forsake them.

That He will be their comforter, and will bring them through every situation they encounter. He will guide them and prepare them to fulfill His plan for their everyday life, and for their future.

BALANCE TIME BETWEEN YOUR HUSBAND AND YOUR KIDS

The relationship between husband and wife must not be neglected. It must not take second place to the time spent caring for the children.

Many times parents build their relationship around the children and neglect their personal relationship with each other.

All their efforts have been for the children, now, they feel they have nothing in common, except the children: who are now grown and gone out on their own and have their own lives to live.

PLEASE DON'T ALLOW THIS TO HAPPEN TO YOUR MARRIAGE.

Raising awesome preacher's kids in the parsonage, on the evangelistic field, or on the mission field, it is our privilege and responsibility to instill the importance of a love for God and His Word, a love for the church, and the ministry into their lives.

Developing their spiritual welfare because, God requires this of us as parents. We show and teach them the Love of God by the way we deal with them and with people.

Most of all the way we cope with and respond to problems or disappointments we encounter. Your kids know when there are family problems and they are especially perceptive of church problems. Don't shut them out! Teach them how to deal with situations and problems of everyday life as they arise.

BOUNDARIES AND RESPONSIBILITIES

We had two foster boys ages nine and twelve.

When they came into our home, they were rebellious and angry. They needed a secure atmosphere, personal attention, and lots of loving care. We loved them and treated them like our own, teaching them by the same standards we taught Debbie. They began to respond.

We set boundaries so they knew what was expected of them:

Gave them responsibilities;
Taught them to complete assigned tasks;
To be in control of their own behavior;
To be accountable for their actions and attitudes;
Gave them *consistent* correction and discipline;
Teaching that there are consequences for bad behavior,
As well as benefits of good behavior.

We also taught spiritual values like:

The importance of a personal relationship with Jesus;
That He loves them unconditionally;
He watches over them;
He wants to be part of their everyday life;
How to develop and establish a consistent prayer life and Bible Study.

We saw changes in their attitudes and their behavior. Their school teachers commented on the changes they saw in the boys.

Parents, your children thrive on your approval. Especially when you complement them for accomplishments with, *"I am so proud of you"* or when you hug them and tell them, *"I love you"*, or when they have done their best, *"good job"*. They need to hear this often from both parents.

Your unconditional love and trust, encourages them to be and to do their best. They must also know that both parents agree on correction and discipline and back each other's decisions, so they don't play one against the other.

IT IS OKAY TO SAY, "NO" TO YOUR KIDS

A young girl began going to visit friends, it led to spending the night, until every day, and every night was spent going and coming. It was as though she was on a merry-go-round and didn't know how to get off.

When her mother stopped her and insisted that she stay home, at first the young girl was very angry. Then it was as though she was relieved that someone had stopped the merry-go-round and made her get off.

CHILDREN NEED CONSISTENT GUIDANCE, CORRECTION AND DISCIPLINE IN ORDER TO FEEL SECURE AND LOVED.

It is so sad that there are some parents who never discipline their children, or say <u>"NO" to them, and mean no!</u>

The child knows that if they cry or continue to plead, that their parents give in to them, and allow them to go and do whatever they want to do.

As a result, those children usually grow up unable to accept responsibility for their actions and attitudes, respect authority, and have a problem taking instruction or training. They tend to blame someone else for their problems.

There is a difference in being their parent, and being their friend. You are their parent with divinely given insights and responsibilities that friends <u>do not have</u>.

Teaching our children not only spiritual values, but skills as well: and how to do for themselves is vitally important.

I appreciated my mother-in-law: she taught her girls and her boys alike in household responsibilities, and skills that would help them when they faced adulthood and life's situations. She prepared them to be good husbands and wives and how to be the best that they could be.

> Proverbs 13:24, "He that spareth his rod hateth his son: but he that loveth him chasteneth him betimes."

We taught Debbie when making decisions, to weigh the cost, and how it would affect her in the future, and that she would have to live with those decisions whether good or bad.

EQUIPPING AND EMPOWERING OUR KIDS PEER PRESSURE AND BULLYING

Dear Parents: Equipping our kids to _SURVIVE_ in their world of peer pressure and bullying is not enough!

Empowering our kids to _THRIVE_ in their world will take: a daily walk with Jesus, making Him the Lord of their life; a consistent Bible Study and prayer life, to establish and to know what they believe; The Baptism of the Holy Spirit to stand firm with spiritual convictions, morals and values. Then they will be equipped and empowered to face and stand up to any situation they encounter.

Peer pressure: Our kids want to be accepted by their peers. They must decide whether or not they will lay aside their principles and values or to stand up for what they know is right.

They must be equipped to make right decisions, to take their stand

and to say no to the peer pressure to smoke, to drink, to do drugs and to say no to sexual permissiveness. In fact, they will become the ones who influence their peers to abstain from those things. They will be world changers!

The Word of God is all powerful. When they know it and know how to apply it to everyday life situations, they can overcome every obstacle that they face. We are raising awesome Christian kids, not only the preacher's kids but the church kids as well.

Kids who have strong morals, values and standards, most of all they will experience the anointing of the Holy Spirit.

They will be the ones who influence the ideals, attitudes and actions of their peers. Our Spirit Filled kids will make a difference in their world and in their schools. Sharing their testimony in the halls, or in the classroom, the power of the Holy Spirit in their lives will help them influence their peers.

NOTE: I have seen kids saved and receive the Baptism in the Holy Spirit in a class room, and in the halls as Spirit filled students share their testimonies. It is time to stop hiding our lights, and being fearful and ashamed.

We are one generation away from God-less-ness in our nation. In fact, look around, are we about there now? It is time to allow God to work through our lives and to make a difference in our schools and see how Jesus can change the lives of our youth and kids from violence to love and care for one another.

Please read: Acts, Chapter 17. *It tells how 12 people changed their world for Jesus. If only 12 disciples could turn their world upside down for God: what can all of us, as Christians do today in our world??? LET'S JUST DO IT!*

Bullying is one of the worse situations kids and adults face today. They are tormented, abused, intimidated and threatened so they will not to tell anyone what is happening to them.

As parents and leaders we must be alert, to any changes in our child's behavior and investigate the reasons for the change. If your child is being bullied or abused, prayerfully seek God for wisdom to help your child to deal with the situation.

When Christian Kids know who they are in Jesus, that they have the Holy Spirit, the anointing and spiritual authority to stand up to their abusers and bullies *in the Name of Jesus.* **They will not be intimidated and with God's help, they will overcome them and can even lead them to Jesus.**

The Bible contains promises for us to stand on and use to overcome any weapon formed against us. Memorizing the scripture until it becomes part of our being provides confidence and authority to claim those promises using them to stop bullies, abusers or any other adversatives encountered.

> *Isaiah 54:17, "No weapon that is formed against thee shall prosper; and every tongue that shall rise against thee in judgment thou shalt condemn. This is the heritage of the servants of the Lord, and their righteousness is in Me," saith the Lord."*

We are not Victims. We are the Victors. We are to be the light of the world, not hiding or being afraid to let our light shine for Jesus. They will become the influence that brings changes in the lives of others when they are Spirit Filled.

> *Matthew 5:14-16. "Ye are the light of the world. A city that is set on an hill cannot be hid."*

V15, "Neither do men light a candle, and put it under a bushel, but on a candlestick; and it giveth light unto all that are in the house."

V16, "<u>Let your light so shine before men, that they may see your good works, and glorify your Father which is in heaven.</u>"

Ephesians 6:10-20, "Finally, my brethren, be strong in the Lord in the power of His might,"

V11, "<u>Put on the whole armor of God, that ye may be able to stand against the wiles of the devil.</u>"

V12, "For we wrestle not against flesh and blood, but against principalities, against powers, against the rulers of the darkness of this world, against spiritual wickedness in high places."

V13, "<u>Wherefore take unto you the whole armor of God, that ye may be able to withstand in the evil day, and having done all, to STAND.</u>"

<u>V14, "STAND THEREFORE,</u> (Knowing and trusting God to fight this battle for you) *having your loins girt about with truth, and having on the breastplate of righteousness;"*

V15, "And your feet shod with the preparation of the Gospel of peace;" (Know the scripture and how and when to use it)

V16, "Above all, taking <u>the shield of faith, wherewith ye shall be able to quench all the fiery darts of the wicked.</u>" (using your faith and trust in God for wisdom to deal with bullies.)

> *V17, "And take the helmet of salvation,* (a helmet protects your mind and thoughts) **and the Sword of the Spirit, which is the Word of God:"**

> *V18, "Praying always with all prayer and supplication in the Spirit, and watching thereunto with all perseverance and supplication for all saints;"*

Scripture gives us boldness to speak as we should, **instead of showing fear, showing holy boldness.** *When we resist the devil, (our adversary) He will have to flee from us. Now, this does not mean that you become the bully!*

> *V19, "And for me that utterance may be given unto me, that I may open my mouth boldly, to make known the mystery of the Gospel."* I can witness to that bully, and lead them to Jesus

> *V20, "For which I am an Ambassador in Bonds:* (I am a representative of God,) **that therein I may speak boldly, as I ought to speak."**

We cannot always be with our kids when they encounter situations where they must make a major choice or decision.

Assure them that God cares about everything that they face. As Spirit filled Christians they have God given power, authority, wisdom, and guidance for each situation. God will help them make good choices, and right decisions. Good choices bring good benefits and good results. Bad choices bring disappointments and the need for correction.

Assure your children that God does NOT: sit up in His heaven watching them, just waiting for them to make a mistake so He can punish them. That is a lie from the devil!

Assure them, that God is indeed watching over them, so they experience His loving presence, which is always with them to love, protect, lead, guide, direct and strengthen them each day, because, He will never leave or forsake them. This is His promise to every child of God.

> *Psalms 91:9-12, 14, 15, "Because thou hast made the Lord, which is my refuge, even the Most High, thy habitation;"*
>
> *V10, "There shall no evil befall thee, neither shall any plague come nigh thy dwelling."* (claim God's promises)
>
> *V11, <u>"For He shall give His angels charge over thee, to keep thee in all thy ways."</u>*
>
> *V12, "They* (His angels) *shall bear thee up in their hands, lest thou dash thy foot against a stone."* (God's protection)
>
> *V14, "Because he hath set his love upon Me, therefore will I deliver him: I will set him on high, because he hath known My Name."*
>
> *V15, <u>"He shall call upon Me, and I will answer him: I will be with him in trouble; I will deliver him, and honor him."</u>*

This is the promise and commitment of our heavenly Father to everyone who has given their all to Him.

NOTE: I have used a lot of scripture in this chapter. When we know God's Word and how to apply it to our lives, NOTHING, or NO ONE can stand against us.

Please prayerfully read each verse and allow it to be applied to your life, your child's life, and your situations. It is so vital that we teach our kids how to pray, to read, and study the Bible, and how to apply it to their everyday life.

These scriptures give us instructions on what we should do, and how we should live our life and claim His promises. We serve an Awesome God, who wants to be involved to guide us in every area of our daily life.

GOD'S COMMANDS TO PARENTS AND LEADERS

Deuteronomy 6:1-9, V1, "Now these are the commandments, the statutes, and the judgments, which the Lord your God commanded to teach you, that ye might do them in the land whither ye go to posses it:"

V2, "That thou mightest fear the Lord thy God, to keep all His statutes and His commandments, which I command thee, thou, and thy son, and thy son's son, all the days of thy life; and that thy days may be prolonged."

V3, "Hear therefore, O Israel, and observe to do it; that it may be well with thee, and that ye may increase mightily, as the Lord God of thy fathers hath promised thee, in the land that floweth with milk and honey."

V4, "Hear, O Israel: the Lord our God is one Lord:"

V5, "And thou shalt love the Lord thy God with thine heart, and with all thy soul, and with all thy might."

V6, "And these words, which I command thee this day, shall be in thine heart:"

V7, "And thou shalt teach them diligently unto thy children, and shalt talk of them when thou sittest in thine house, and when thou walkest by the way, and when thou liest down, and when thou risest up."

V8, "And thou shalt bind them for a sign upon thine hand, and they shall be as frontlets between thine eyes."

V9, "And thou shalt write them upon the posts of thy house, and on thy gates."

<u>**NOTE: This sounds like God intends for us to take these scriptures and seriously apply them to our lives, and the lives of our children.**</u>

Think about it: if we obey these scriptures, what a difference it will make in our families, in our churches and in our world!

Proverbs 22:6, "Train up a child in the way he should go: and when he is old, he will not depart from it."

What you have instilled in them will sustain them and help to determine their spiritual relationship with God, and how they will survive and thrive in this sinful world we live in.

NOTE: The Disciples were with Jesus all the time. They saw the need to be taught a consistent prayer life. How much more as parents and leaders do we need to have a consistent prayer life to make us strong in the Lord, so we can teach our children?

Luke 11:1, "And it came to pass, that, as He was praying in a certain place, when He ceased, one of His disciples said unto Him, "Lord, teach us to pray, as John also taught his disciples."

Praying with your children, instructing them how to pray, and that God hears and answers their prayers is one of our greatest ministries. Prayer is simply talking to God, and listening for God to reveal His will and His answer to our prayer.

Recently a Dad told me that when he prays, his three year old repeats every word he hears. Children are imitators; they will repeat what they hear. Children learn by the example their parents and leaders set before them.

A child is never too young to accept Jesus as Savior. When they acknowledge their need to be saved we have the privilege of leading them to a personal relationship with Jesus. We never discount a child's spiritual experiences, encounters, or visions.

When and if a child tells you that God is calling them into the ministry, encourage them to listen to God, and obey His prompting in their lives. Help them develop the talents and gifts God has given to them.

Encourage them to dedicate everything to Jesus, and not let anything or anyone hinder what God is placing in their hearts for them to be and to do. Many of our preachers, preacher's wives, and missionaries were called to ministry when they were children.

> *Luke 18:16, "But Jesus called them unto Him, and said, "Suffer the little children to come unto Me, and forbid them not, for of such is the kingdom of God."*

If there is any doubt, that God uses very young children, we are pointed to *1 Samuel Chapter 1 and Chapter 3.*

NOTE: When Samuel was weaned, (a toddler) his mother brought him to the house of the Lord at Shiloh and presented him to the Lord and to Eli the priest as she had promised God. From that point, as a little child Samuel, ministered before the Lord.

> *1 Samuel 3:10, "And <u>the Lord came, and stood, and called as at other times, "Samuel, Samuel." Then Samuel answered, "Speak; for Thy servant heareth."</u>*

In Verses 11-18, The Lord spoke to Samuel, as a child, with a judgment message for the priest, which he delivered to Eli.

> *V19, "And Samuel grew, and the Lord was with him, and did let none of his words fall to the ground."* (what a promise)

> *V20, "And all Israel from Dan even to Beersheba knew that Samuel was established to be a prophet of the Lord."*

WHAT ABOUT THOSE HARD QUESTIONS?

By all means, teach your children to come to you with all their questions, even those hard ones about drugs, drinking, smoking, sex, and honesty.

Don't be shocked, or embarrassed to answer questions when they ask them. Start when they are little, when they first become inquisitive, explaining what they need to know at each age level.

If we fail to answer their questions and teach them godly scriptural morals and values, they will learn them from others, and most likely, by the worlds standards and not by God's standards.

These scriptures deal with the penalty for committing sexual sin. This seems to be one of the downfalls of young people today. They must know what the Bible says about permissiveness for their own spirituality and protection.

God created sex for marriage only. The Bible Says: those who are sexually active before marriage will not enter heaven, unless they ask God for forgiveness, and abstain until married.

It is just as important for boys to be virgins, as it is for girls to be virgins, to abstain from sexual activity until marriage.

1 Corinthians 6:9-10, "Know ye not that the unrighteous <u>shall not inherit the Kingdom of God?</u> Be not deceived: neither fornicators, nor idolaters, nor adulterers, nor effeminate, nor abusers of themselves with mankind,"

V10, "Nor thieves, nor covetous, nor drunkards, nor revilers, nor extortioners, shall inherit the kingdom of God."

DEFINITIONS:

(Fornicators = having sexual intercourse outside of marriage)

(Idolaters = worshipers of idols)

(Adulterers = sexual intercourse by a married person with Anyone, other than their spouse)

(Effeminate, =sex changes: a woman to an UN-man, a man to an UN-woman; transgender-)

(Homosexual and Lesbian = abusers of themselves with mankind = sexual relations men with men, or women with women.

1 Corinthians 6: 18-20, "<u>Flee fornication,</u> every sin that a man doeth is without the body; but he that <u>committeth fornication sinneth against his own body."</u>

V19, "What, know ye not that your body is the temple of the Holy Ghost which is in you, which ye have of God, and ye are not your own?"

V20, "For ye are bought with a price: therefore glorify God in your body, and in your Spirit, which are God's."

GOD, IS PERFECT, HE DOES NOT MAKE MISTAKES.

In our perverse world, our children and youth as well as adults, are bombarded with stories promoting:

Young girls and women thinking they are really a boy or man trapped in a girl's or woman's body, Young boys or men thinking they are really a girl or woman trapped in a boy or man's body.

They say that God made a mistake when they were born and that it is okay to have sex changes. This is contrary to God's Word. It is a lie from Satan to deceive and destroy God's human creation.

NOTE: *These are difficult areas to deal with, however, if we the parents and the church fail to confront them the world will be glad to! How will our children know what God says about these things if we don't teach and prepare them?*

A GOOD MOTTO TO FOLLOW IS:

"I will put nothing in my life today that will bring me trouble, heartache, sorrow or regret tomorrow. I will live my life every day to please God, so I will have no regrets; so the Devil has nothing to torment me with, or to accuse me of."

CLAIMING GOD'S PROMISES

Every Promise in the Bible is ours. We have not because we ask not and sometimes we ask amiss.

God watches over us because He loves us. He is always with us to help us resist temptation. Our faith in God will see us through any situation or problem when we trust His word and claim His promises for ourselves.

Debbie was very sick. She had the German measles and the mumps at the same time. Her fever went to 106 degrees. The doctor said if her fever would go down to 101 degrees, in the next two hours she would not have to go to the hospital.

We called our church to prayer on her behalf. We asked them to pray that her fever would go down to 101 degrees. Well, in a short time, her fever went down to 101 degrees just what we asked for. As I think about our prayer request, I ask myself,

"Why didn't we ask God to heal her completely?"

She was still very sick. One day, a knock came on the door. When I answered it, there was a lady that I did not know. She had a beautiful quilt in her hands. She said,

"God told me that the pastor's little girl was very ill. That I should make this quilt, pray over it, and bring it to you with the instructions for you to place it on your child, and God will heal her. Now, this quilt is only material and thread but there is a promise, and an anointing God has placed on it."

I thanked her, and invited her in, she told me she had completed her mission and turned to go.

I watched as she walked away and suddenly she was gone. I inquired about this woman and no one in our town knew her.

The Bible tells us that God has given His angels charge over us to keep us in all our ways, and that we sometimes entertain angels unawares. I am sure that I entertained an angel that day.

Psalms 91: 9-11, "Because thou hast made the Lord, which is my refuge, even the Most High, thy habitation;"

> *V10, "There shall no evil befall thee, neither shall any plague come nigh thy dwelling."*

> *V11, "For He shall give His angels charge over thee, to keep thee in all thy ways."*

I took that quilt and placed it on Debbie. Immediately, her fever broke and she was healed. God's promise was fulfilled.

Through the years, whenever she was ill, I placed that quilt on her (*as a point of contact*), asking God for her healing, and she quickly recovered not from the quilt, but by the promise, and anointing of The Holy Spirit.

(This is the same principal the Bible speaks of in Acts 19, regarding the use of prayer cloths.)

> **Acts 19:11-12, *"And God wrought special miracles at the hands of Paul:"***

> **V12, *"So that from his body were brought unto the sick handkerchiefs or aprons, and the diseases departed from them, and the evil spirits went out of them."***

LIFE IS NOT ALWAYS FAIR

There have been occasions when ministers and their families have been severely hurt by the actions and attitudes of individuals in the church or by a congregation. Some situations were so devastating that ministers have even left the ministry.

NOTE: Our children are taught by our example. They learn to cope with and overcome their problems by watching how you and I react and how we deal with each other.

One cannot allow any root of bitterness to grow in your mind or in your heart. It only hurts you and it will destroy you and your ministry if you give into it.

Hebrews 12:15, "Looking diligently lest any man fail of the grace of God; lest any root of bitterness springing up trouble you, and thereby many be defiled:"

NOTE: Your children are watching how you react in every situation. You are teaching them by your actions and your attitudes. They will learn more; establish their habits, attitudes, and values from what you do, than from what you say!

KEEP ON HOLDING ON

And *IF*, after all your love, training and praying, your children turns their back on God, and all you have instilled in them,

KEEP ON HOLDING ON TO GOD'S PROMISES! You have dedicated them to Him. They are His, and The Holy Spirit will continually bring conviction to their heart. Keep on holding on and interceding on their behalf.

NOTE: *Place them on the altar and trust God's promises. Keep raising them up before God in prayer. Whatever their choices, they are accountable for them. You have fulfilled your place in their lives. Now they will make their own decisions and God will hold them accountable for their choices. God's promise to you is:*

Proverbs 22:6, "Train up a child in the way he should go: and when he is old, *HE WILL NOT DEPART FROM IT!"*

NOTE: *Know this that the spiritual training you have instilled in them will never leave them. They may not live as you think they should but deep down in their hearts they can never get away from their spiritual training, and the prayers of their parents.*

Take Heart: and because of your faithfulness and your prayers, the Holy Spirit will continue to influence them to return to their roots, and once again have that personal relationship with Jesus.

FAMILY SUPPER TIME

Day after day, today's busy families pass each other, coming and going. **They may sit in the same room together yet instead of talking they are texting.**

A great way to cement family relationships is for every member of the family to set down to at least one meal a day together with, **No TV... or... No phones.** Think of it as "Family Table Time" when everyone shares events of their day, their thoughts, problems, desires and dreams.

One of the most treasured memories of my childhood was our family supper time. Each of us had our time to talk about our day. We listened to each other, and most of all our parents listened to each of us. They would give wise instruction, counsel, encouragement, correction and discipline when needed. That relationship stayed with me through all my life.

WHAT ABOUT THOSE AWESOME CHURCH KIDS?

NOTE: *It is not only about the kids in the parsonage, it is about all those kids and youth in the church as well. Good Sunday school teachers, Children and Youth leaders only have an hour or two each week to teach and train them spiritually.*

Children spend most of their time in the home with their parents. Some choose not to teach their children about God: others choose to leave spiritual matters up to the church.

A teenager in our church was giving her parents a lot of problems. They asked us to council her in spiritual matters. It did not take long to realize that she had very little knowledge of the Bible, or a spiritual foundation to stand on. **She knew what she didn't believe in and what she didn't do.**

Her parents had just expected her to have adequate spiritual knowledge since she was raised in the church and in a Christian home.

How sad, that this is the story of so many young people who have grown up in our churches and Christian homes. They have acquired very little spiritual foundations to stand on. When they face temptations they can be swayed and influenced to go the way of the world, and many times end up away from God and the church.

*As **church leaders**, we must do our part to teach and train our kids and youth, as well as helping parents understand the importance of their GOD GIVEN RESPONSIBILITY, and their part in the spiritual training and guidance of their children in the home. The Bible gives instructions to parents and leaders,*

> *Deuteronomy 6:4-9 and 11:18-20, V5, "And thou shalt love the Lord thy God with all thine heart, and with all thy soul and with all thy might."*
>
> *V6, "And these words, which I command thee this day, shall be in thine heart:"*
>
> *V7, "And thou shalt teach them diligently unto thy children, and shall talk of them when thou sittest in thine house, and when thou walkest by the way, and when thou liest down, and when thou risest up."*

Proverbs 22:6, "Train up a child in the way he should go: and when he is old, he will not depart from it."

We accept the challenge that together with their parents, we are raising up strong Christian youth and children both in the preacher's home, and in the church and in church family homes. Fully spiritually equipping them to stand firm in their faith, knowing what they believe, and prepared to be victorious Christians in their daily lives. We owe it to each of them!

I appreciate a parent who is teaching his children spiritual truths and values. His son at age seven accepted Jesus as his personal Savior. He loved to read his Bible. He asked to be baptized in water.

His dad told their pastor that his son wanted to be baptized in water. The pastor told the Dad, that the child was too young to understand what it meant and chose not to baptize the child.

HOW SAD. This child was denied this experience. It left a negative impact on his spiritual life. It is so important that we are sensitive to the spiritual needs, growth and development of our children and youth. We cannot fail our kids and our youth!

IT TAKES TEAM WORK

Church leaders and parents, working together, raising and teaching our children and youth to fulfill God's plan for their life, will equip them to take their places in leadership, in business, in schools, in government, and in our churches, as pastors, pastor's wives, missionaries, evangelists and teachers.

They will establish godly families, preparing the next generation of awesome kids and youth to be the godly leaders of the future, and the church: continues to fulfill its purpose and its mission. AMEN AND AMEN!

SOMETHING TO THINK ABOUT

WHAT IF: God chooses to call one of your children or youth to be a missionary on some foreign mission field? How would you react? Would you willing commit that child to God and encourage them to accept God's Call?

I thought: *what if,* God chose to call Debbie to be His missionary to some faraway place? She had a heart for missions. She had gone on several Youth Aim Trips to minister in other countries.

MY RESPONSE WAS: that I loved having her close. Yet, if God had chosen to call her as His missionary that, I would rather see her thousands of miles away, on some foreign field _IN GOD'S WILL_ with His protection and guidance in her life.

Then, for her to be setting in my house knowing that she was _OUT OF GOD'S WILL_ not fulfilling God's purpose and plan for her life. She fulfilled His plan for her life and He called her to her heavenly home. forever to be in His presence.

More and more God is calling our children and youth to take their place as spiritual leaders in churches, missions, evangelism, and other areas of ministry.

He is also preparing them to take their place in key positions as Christian leaders in today's society, in schools, in government, in communities, in business, and medical fields.

We have the privilege and responsibility to continue training our children and youth to follow God whether they are called to ministry, or chosen to be faithful followers of our Lord Jesus.

We have this confidence that we are raising "Awesome Kids and Youth" who are taking their place, making a difference in this troubled world, and that God will do His part to lead, guide, and direct them.

Chapter 6

DEALING WITH DIFFICULT SITUATIONS

THROUGH IT ALL

Through all the years of our ministry God has always sustained us. Sometimes He worked through our family and friends. Other times it was as though God sheltered us in a place like He did for Moses.

When the children of Israel rose up against him, God placed him in the "Clift of the Rock" and covered him there with His hand allowing him to see His Glory.

Through it all dear preacher's wife, take heart. No matter what comes or what goes, know that God has promised that He will never leave or forsake you. When you go through hard places or troubled times, He is there to sustain you. Take hold of His nail scarred hand, and stand on His promises given in,

> *PSALMS 23:1-6, "The Lord is my shepherd; I shall not want."*
>
> *V2, "He maketh me to lie down in green pastures: He leadeth me beside still waters."*

V3, "He restoreth my soul: He leadeth me in the paths of righteousness for His Name's sake."

V4, "Yea, though I walk through the valley of the shadow of death, I will fear no evil: for Thou art with me; Thy Rod and Thy Staff they comfort me."

V5, "Thou preparest a table before me in the presence of mine enemies: Thou anointest my head with oil; my cup runeth over."

V6, "Surely goodness and mercy shall follow me all the days of my life: and I will dwell in the house of the Lord forever."

God is always on time, He is never late, and He will take you through every fiery furnace trial and life-storm you face. Remember you are God's Chosen Vessel!

Acts 9:15, "But the Lord said unto him, "Go thy way: for he is a chosen vessel unto Me, to bear My Name before the Gentiles, and kings, and the Children of Israel:"

Psalms 17:8, "Keep me as the apple of the eye, hide me under the shadow of Thy Wings."

Psalms 30:5, "For His Anger endureth but a moment; in His Favor is life: weeping may endure for a night, but joy cometh in the morning."

PERFECT HARMONY

It would be awesome, if there was always perfect harmony in the family and in the church. **From time to time**, there will be situations arise which must be dealt with, some in fervent prayer others with wisdom and diplomacy.

Ever heard these comments? People of this church are not friendly, no one spoke to me, and no one shook my hand, or I m going where I can be fed. Then there are those, who criticize the song service, the music is too loud, or the preacher preaches too long on and on.

God will give you the wisdom, to give an answer to them. Sometimes, it is best to keep silent and just saturate the situation in prayer. And as always the Bible says in,

Proverbs 15:1, "A soft answer turns away wrath: but grievous words stir up anger."

EACH CHURCH AND EACH PASTOR HAS A PERSONALITY AND A REPUTATION

Personality defined: *A characteristic way of thinking or feeling, behavior, moods, attitudes, opinions, qualities, openness, admiration, conscientiousness, agreeable or disagreeable.*

Reputation defined: *The opinion that people have about someone or something. How much admiration and respect is based on past behavior or character. The reputation of a church or individual depends on their actions and attitudes.*

What a blessing when personalities and reputations manifest godly characteristics. When a church or individual has a bad reputation, it both precedes and follows them hindering their growth, influence, purpose and the ability to reach the lost.

At a General Council meeting, ministers, missionaries and delegates from around the world gather to be refreshed, fellowship and conduct business. Each wore a badge with their name and place of ministry. We proudly wore ours. As people greeted us and saw where we pastored, they would say,

"Oh, you pastor that church with the demon deacon board."

What a shock! It made us wonder what we were in for. How sad, to think a church would have this kind of reputation.

The church is to be a lighthouse to the community. A place where the love of God is preached, and practiced, where the lost would be saved, the sick receive healing, people who are struggling to be set free, and a haven of rest for broken people to be restored.

This church God smiles on, because it is fulfilling the purpose God intended for His church. That is, to reach the lost, and for the perfecting of the saints.

HIS CHURCH IS NOT A BUILDING

HIS CHURCH is not made of wood or stone, brick and mortar.

HIS CHURCH is made up of born again believers from all people groups, cultures, and races who have accepted Jesus as their personal Savior. We are one in unity and love for God and one another. If one member is suffering the others gather around to comfort, encourage and help them.

People will be attracted to this church from all walks of life. They will experience a friendly family atmosphere, anointed music, worship and preaching of God's Word.

Most of all they will sense the presence of the Holy Spirit that dwells in and among those who worship in that building. People will grow and develop spiritually.

The next generation of leaders will be trained to continue the ministry of His church.

People who are hungry for God, those who are lost, and those who are looking for a church home will be drawn to this church.

In His church there will be various areas and imperfections among those attending. In reality there was only one who was perfect, that was Christ Jesus Himself. His church will include those who are born again believers and those who have received the baptism of the Holy Spirit.

HIS CHURCH WILL LIKELY INCLUDE

Some People who are unbelievers
Some individuals whose doctrine is incorrect
Some may even have a critical or a fault finding spirit,
Some who tend to cause conflict or division,
Some live from crisis to crisis,
Some who demand their own way,
Some who seek or hold their position,
Some may get on your last nerve,
Some who seem to enjoy spreading rumors.

The possibility of one or two of those being in your congregation is likely. How will you deal with them as you lead the flock that God has entrusted into your care?

First of all, pray for godly wisdom to help each person. If, they are teachable, teach them. If they are in positions of leadership it may be necessary to confront them with love and counsel them. Pray with them to get on a right path. Apostle Paul writes in,

> **Romans 16:17-20, "Now I beseech you, brethren, mark them which cause divisions and offenses contrary to the doctrine which ye have learned; and avoid them."**
>
> **V18, "For they that are such serve not our Lord Jesus**

Christ, but their own belly; and by good words and fair speeches deceive the hearts of the simple."

V19, "For your obedience is come abroad unto all men. I am glad therefore on your behalf: but yet I would have you wise unto that which is good, and simple concerning evil."

V20, "And the God of peace shall bruise Satan under your feet shortly. The grace of our Lord Jesus Christ be with you. Amen."

Prayerfully seek God for guidance, wisdom and direction for each situation and for the perfecting of the saints in preparation for the soon coming of our Lord Jesus Christ.

WHY CONGREGATIONS AND PASTORS CLASH?

Each pastor, pastor's wife, and church has a personality. When the personality of the pastor and the personality of the church are not compatible, it is likely that the two will have problems.

It does not mean that the pastor is bad, or that the church is bad, however, both can get a bad reputation which neither deserves. For this reason, when pastoral changes are being made: both congregation and minister should become acquainted with each other's personality and methods of leadership so they are compatible. Most of all seeking God's will to be done.

Sometimes there are individuals who decide they just want a change in pastors. Instead of a prayer meeting to seek God's will and His plan for the future, some may decide that they just want to change pastors.

How heartless and thoughtless. At election time, they vote and the pastor is not re-elected. This is devastating to both the church and most of all to the pastor's family. It can destroy the minister and his family and possibly divide the church family. Some have lost out with God. Some recover, and some may not.

NOTE: *If and when facing a circumstance such as this, one must allow the Holy Spirit to bring inner healing, comfort and strength to overcome the hurt one experiences.*

Please don't allow any root of bitterness to hinder or destroy you, your family or your ministry. It is sometimes hard to forgive those who have wounded you. Jesus tells us that we must forgive that our Father in heaven may forgive us. If we will not forgive, neither will our heavenly Father forgive us our trespasses. These are the words of Jesus.

> **Mark 11:25-26, "And when ye stand praying, forgive, if ye have ought against any: that your Father which is in heaven may forgive your trespasses."**

> **V26, "But if ye do not forgive, neither will your Father also which is in heaven forgive your trespasses."**

If you leave a pastorate with hurt, and anger, you take it with you. It will follow you, and will only increase next time you have a problem. This kind of baggage can destroy you, your ministry and your family. You end up in a self imposed prison with bitterness which will destroy you, unless you deal with it.

LET GO OF YOUR BAGGAGE!

Everyone has likely experienced disappointments, losses, hurts, and wounded spirits, during their lifetime. If, we do not forgive and deal with it, we only allow the baggage of bitterness, strife, and anger to dominate our lives.

The longer we carry it, the bigger it grows, and the heavier it becomes. We dwell on how someone hurt us or what someone did and wonder why we are so miserable.

Perhaps you have been disappointed, let down or have experienced great loss. Things may happen that are beyond our control. How we react and deal with them will determine the happiness or despair of our lives. If we allow them to build they will enslave us until we become locked in a prison of our own making.

Danny, was saved, baptized in the Holy Spirit and called into the ministry. He loved singing and preaching revivals. People were saved, healed and delivered.

A person in leadership proceeded to embarrass him publically telling him that he just thought he was called to preach. This person continued to discourage, criticize and put him down.

Danny was so deeply hurt and discouraged he lost heart and turned away from the ministry and the church. He began drinking and running with the wrong crowd. He carried this baggage for many years.

I sat beside him in a church service one Sunday night. The pastor had preached about "Forgiveness and Carrying Your Baggage" and was making his altar call. I turned to Danny and said,

"Don't you think that you have carried your baggage long enough? You are bitter, and unforgiving, and it is destroying you".

"Don't you think it is time to place it on the altar, give it all to Jesus, to walk away and leave it there?"

"Ask God to forgive you and take you back. He will help you to forgive that person who hurt you and you can leave here tonight a free man."

Danny, went to the altar, placed all his baggage there, rededicated his life and asked God to forgive him and to heal his brokenness. He purposed in his heart to forgive that one who had wounded him. That night he left his sin and bitterness on the altar.

At home, He told his family that he loved them and promised them that there would be no more drinking. He was a changed man when he let go of the baggage he had carried for so many years. God opened the doors of the prison he had made for himself, and he walked out a free man.

When we hold un-forgiveness, anger and bitterness in our hearts, we are the ones who suffer. The person or persons, who wounded us, GOES FREE! It doesn't bother them that you are hurt or eat up with bitterness.

You may feel that they don't deserve forgiveness, but you deserve to be free. We must allow God to deal with them. They will give an account to God and He will judge accordingly. Life is too short to allow anything, or anyone to destroy our peace or happiness.

We must learn to pack up the trouble, and lay it on the altar walk away, leaving it there. ***Never go back and take it up again.***

NOTE: *One may think, I will forgive, but I won't forget what they did. It is true these situations will be in your memory bank. There are times when you may relive the situation. That is only Satan trying to torment and weigh you down again with that old baggage. Just say,*

"No Satan, I have already dealt with that. I left it all on the altar and I am set free from that baggage. You have no power or right to bring it up to me again. "So STOP now, in Jesus' Name."

PROTECTING YOUNG MINISTERS

As leaders we are to encourage and help young ministers. As they develop and mature, provide opportunities for them to minister. When my husband first began in ministry, pastors would say,

"Brother Hill, when you get more experience, I will invite you to preach for me." Bill would think:

"How will I get more experience if I don't have opportunities to preach?

When He became a pastor, he made sure he invited young preachers to fill the pulpit. He would say to the congregation,

"I have invited a young preacher just starting out in ministry to come and preach to us. I know you will encourage him. One of these days, when he is successful you will know that he preached some of his first sermons in your church, and that you helped him get his start in the ministry."

I must say, there were times! One young preacher walked back and forth across the platform, for over thirty minutes wringing his hands and saying,

"Stand up for Jesus! Stand up for Jesus! People, stand up for Jesus!"

That was the total of his sermon. Our people would say,

"Amen brother preach it."

And later, when he had matured, they were pleased that they had encouraged him and had a part in his growth and development.

I have known young ministers who have been deeply hurt and

wounded by a spiritual leader they have served with as Youth and Children's Pastors, Worship Leaders and Staff.

As spiritual leaders we must use godly wisdom and love in the way we treat, deal with, and provide for those who minister along side of us.

God will hold us accountable for the way we treat one another.

What joy and privilege it is to be a mentor and witness the growth and development of a young preacher.

WHEN GOD SAYS, "IT IS TIME TO MOVE ON!"

Pastor and pastor's wife you will know when you have completed God's assignment and He releases you to move on to your next "THERE PLACE".

Leave in good standing with a good attitude and spirit. Assure the congregation that God has called you to another place of ministry. Thank them for all they have meant to you. Pray that God will send another shepherd to lead them in the next phase of their spiritual growth.

HOW DO I LOVE SOMEONE WHO REFUSES TO LOVE ME?

The Apostle Paul in his letter to the church at Rome gives instructions as to how one is to deal with this situation. One should read Romans Chapter 12 to get the full answer to this question. The Bible says,

> **Romans 12:20-21, *"Therefore if thine enemy hunger, feed him; if he thirst, give him drink: for in so doing thou shalt heap coals of fire on his head."***

(I don't think this means to literally set him on fire!)

> *Verse 21, "Be not overcome of evil, but overcome evil with good."*

We can take a lesson from Jesus Himself. He came to His own and His own received Him not. He was despised and rejected by His own. Yet, it did not change Him or His purpose, His love or His provisions for them or His ministry to them.

> *Isaiah 53:3-5, "He is despised and rejected of men; a man of sorrows, and acquainted with grief: and we hid as it were our faces from Him; He was despised, and we esteemed Him not."*

> *V4, "Surely He hath borne our griefs, and carried our sorrows: yet we did esteem Him stricken, smitten of God and afflicted."*

> *V5, "But He was wounded for our transgressions, He was bruised or our iniquities: the chastisement of our peace was upon Him; and with His stripes we are healed."*

> *John 1:10-12, "He was in the world, and the world was made by Him, and the world knew Him not."*

> *V11, "He came unto His own, and His own received Him not."*

> *V12, "But as many as received Him, to them gave He power to become the sons of God, even to them that believed on His Name."*

I WAS A YOUNG PASTOR'S WIFE

We had only been the pastors of this congregation for two or three weeks. We were still getting acquainted with the people and learning all their names.

On Sunday morning we were greeting the people as they arrived. A lady came in, and began telling me how terrible I was. She really let me have it. All that day, I had myself a pity party. I questioned,

"Why did she do this to me? I hardly know her name I have not been here long enough to do anything to offend her."

I got over it, until the next time, because it happened, again and again, and again. By this time, it was really getting to me. I really struggled with this. I could not understand why she was continually accosting me. I knew if I tried to deal with it we would probably have to leave that pastorate.

I continued to ask God to help me understand her actions and her attitude so I could resolve this situation.

I inquired about her and her family. She and her husband had been in the ministry, and that he left her for a young pastor's wife. This put her out of the ministry, and left her with children to raise by herself. When things would overcome her, she would lash out at one who represented her pain: another young pastor's wife, (ME). I cried out,

"Lord, all she has to do is ask, I would be glad to help her."

He let me know that she couldn't ask because she may not realize the reason she is doing it. I said,

"OKAY God, let her get me again, I'm ready for her."

The next time she went off on me, I told her it was okay, that I understood and for us to just have a word of prayer. I placed my arms around her, and began praying for her. She resisted, but I continued to pray for her.

"Lord, this is your child and You know all about her situation. I ask You to supply her every need and help her through this difficult time."

"Bless her now with comfort and peace in her heart and her family. I ask this in Your Name Jesus. Thank You Lord, for Your blessing on her life and her family. AMEN."

I thought, that takes care of that. Actually I was a little proud of myself. However, she continued to do it. Each time, I just told her it was okay, that I understood, and said,

"Let's just have that word of prayer."

Placed my arms around her, and began praying for her. It took a *whole year* praying with her, before she was finally able to come to me and say,

"Sister Hill, could we just have that word of prayer?"

I was no longer the enemy and a precious relationship developed between the two of us.

NOTE: *We must keep in our hearts and minds that our real enemy is not one another, it is Satan, who is going to and fro across the land, seeking whom he may devour.*

Please don't let it be YOU, SISTER PREACHER'S WIFE! Or, YOU, SISTER WOMAN IN MINISTRY!

God sent us there for this dear lady, to help her through such a devastating time in her life. Think about it. God may have brought us to this place especially for her. That is how important each soul is to God.

Just as God looked beyond our faults, and saw our need, sometimes we need to stop, take a look at what may or may not be going on in the lives of others, and minister to them. After all, we were called there to minister to ALL the people in that congregation and to that community.

WAR BETWEEN THE SAINTS

The story goes that there were two ladies in a church who were at war with each other. This could probably happen in any church. This had gone on for a very long time. They sat on opposite sides of the church glaring at each other. The pastor had prayed for some time about the situation.

One morning as he was preparing for service, he told God he had had it with those two and he had decided that he would deal with it that day. God seemed to say,

"Is that right?"

The pastor replied,

"I have made up my mind I am going to settle this war today!"

At this point, God assured the preacher that this was His business and He would take care of the problem in His own time and in His own way.

One Sunday, during the altar service, the pastor noticed those two ladies had knelt on opposite ends of the altar. As he watched, both got up from the altar and started for each other looking rather determined.

He thought, oh no, they are going to fight right here in front of God and everybody. When they met face to face, they started crying, hugged each other, and both ask the other to forgive them.

Revival broke out in that church. Some things just need to be saturated in prayer, and allow God to take care of His business, in His own way and in His own time.

ACCEPTING CRITICISM GRACEFULLY

There may be times when you are criticized for something you had done, planned or preached, or for something that you had nothing to do with. Like the lady I referred to earlier. Pray that the Holy Spirit would give you wisdom to handle each situation so it will be resolved.

Those in the ministry should not carry their feelings or a chip on their shoulder, because someone may be there ready to knock it off!

> **PROVERBS 15:1, "A soft answer turneth away wrath: but grievous words stir up anger."**

NOTE: you will not please everyone all the time. Just do your best to walk with God, and to please Him, and when or if criticism comes, ask God for wisdom to handle it **gracefully.**

REASONS PEOPLE CRITICIZE

There may be times when "you" need a reality check.
There is such a thing as helpful criticism.
They are asking for help.
They are jealous or envious of your position.
They want to let you know they are displeased with something.
They just don't like you,

They don't like something your husband or you had done or preached.

They just simply have a critical spirit

They are afraid of losing their position.

They are trying to see how far they can go.

They just want to hurt someone because they hurt.

There are so many more reasons and excuses for people lashing out at you: "The Preacher's Wife" or "The Woman in Ministry".

COMMUNICATION WITH YOUR AUDIENCE:

When one is in a position of leadership, it is easy for a misunderstanding to occur.

Even when explaining in detail a project, or a position, there may be some who will not visualize what you are presenting. I learned to consider my audience.

As a Pastor's wife, or a lady minister, you most likely have a variety of age levels, cultures, and backgrounds, to consider.

"PERCEPTION" One must evaluate how your audience will *"PERCEIVE" what you are planning, or speaking about. Use words, thoughts and terms that your audience will readily comprehend and thus understand your message.*

Consider in scripture: when Jesus was teaching His followers, He recognized that they were from all walks of life and all ages. For this reason, He spoke to them in parables, stories, and things He knew they could relate with and understand.

He kept His messages simple. He taught with a dual purpose. He knew that some would grasp the spiritual message He was expressing to them. He also knew that others would only hear His stories.

As a preacher, preacher's wife, women in ministry, leadership, a Bible teacher, Sunday school teacher, etc. you will likely be more effective when planning an event, expressing your thoughts or opinions when you carefully consider: how what you do, or what you say will be **PERCEIVED** by those you are speaking too.

Perceived defined: How it will be received, understood and accepted or rejected by those you are speaking too.

This could determine the success or failure of what you are presenting. It could also help to prevent misunderstandings and conflicts.

A GIFT FOR TWO SISTERS

Communicating Christian love makes a difference. We made contact with a large family in our community. We invited two of the sisters to our girls program called Missionettes. They started coming to Missionettes, and attended church services as well.

Now these two little girls would fight over anything. If one looked at the other, and she didn't like what she saw, she would get up in service, go across pews and the fight was on.

Some of our ladies came to me and suggested that we encourage them to go to the church down the street. That they were dirty, used bad language, and disturbed services.

This broke my heart. I suggested that two of them, would take an interest in the sisters, purchase a small gift, wrap it up, and ask one of the sisters to sit with them and that they should separate them by sitting on different sides of the church.

During the service, they should slip their arm around their girl, and tell her that Jesus loves her and that they love her too, then present the little gift to her. **I *perceived*** that they were not interested in my proposal.

The next Sunday, I was at the piano I looked back for the girls. I saw two of those ladies, each with a sister sitting beside her, one on each side of the church.

I watched as service progressed, each one slipped their arm around their girl, spoke to her, and presented her with their little gift.

Can you imagine how I felt? I saw each little girl look up at her lady with such love. After church, I looked for those ladies to thank them. When I met them, each had their girl by the hand. With tears in their eyes, they related how blessed they were to have made friends with their girl. They continued to mentor those two sisters.

Years passed, we were no longer pastoring that church. Someone knocked on my door, when I opened it there stood a beautiful well dressed young woman. I greeted her and invited her to come in.

When she told me her name I immediately recognized that it was one of the two sisters. She proceeded to show pictures of her husband, her home and little children, all very well kept. I asked, if she was still going to church. She said,

"Oh yes, we never miss a service or activity. I am the Missionettes leader ministering to little girls like I was when that lady asked me to sit by her and presented me with a gift. She told me she loved me, and that Jesus loved me too."

NOTE: *What if, we had turned those two sisters away? Perhaps that whole family would have been lost and spent eternity in a devil's hell.* **Think about all those little girls she was reaching for Jesus.**

We never know what plans God has for that child or even that adult that seems to disrupt everything.

Every person that God brings to your church has potential. He has a plan for their lives, and gives you an opportunity to be part of that plan. Young or old, rich or poor, it is our privilege to nurture them, and point them to Jesus. Leave it to God to fulfill His plan in their lives.

THAT REMINDS ME OF ANOTHER YOUNG GIRL I KNOW. She was known as the terror of her neighborhood.

A neighbor invited her to go with them to a revival at their church. That night she committed her life to Jesus. Later the question was asked, about the results of that revival. They said,

"Only a rag-a-muffin kid was saved"

I AM, THAT RAG-A-MUFFIN KID!

They did not know the Plan
God had in store for my life and my future!

TIMES WHEN YOUR HEART BREAKS

There were two young couples with family connections to our church. Two brothers had married two sisters. Both couples were expecting a new baby. Each gave birth about the same time. One couple's baby was stillborn. The other couple was surprised with not one baby but two. They had twins.

The couple with the stillborn baby could not understand why they would leave the hospital with no baby, and their Brother and Sister would leave the hospital taking home two babies.

NOTE: *How do you go from one room celebrating and congratulating this couple with two beautiful babies, and then enter the next room where their brother and sister was suffering so great a loss.*

What could we say that will bring comfort to them? There was no pat answer to their question of: why this had happened to them. We sought God for wisdom.

We assured them that God loved them. That He was the healer of broken hearts. We prayed that the Holy Spirit would be with them continually to comfort and help them as they faced each day and long nights ahead.

We assured them that we have this hope of being reunited with loved ones and that their precious little one would be waiting for them in heaven.

NOTE: There will likely be times when tragedies strike. It could be loss of loved ones, jobs, health, homes, or finances. Prayerfully seek God, that He will give you the wisdom, and strength to cope with each situation.

Be careful with the use of well known catch phrases like:

These catch phrases mean little to grieving loved ones.

> He or she is better off
> God took your loved one
> He or she will not suffer any more
> God knows best
> They are in a better place
> Everything happens for a reason

In fact, they may tend to cause the family to be angry with God for their loss. Use encouraging terms like:

God loves you. He will see you through.
God will make a way where there seems to be no way.
He is Faithful. You can trust Him and His promises.
God will supply all your needs.
God will strengthen and comfort you.
God will open doors for you.
God's Promises are to you.
He will never leave you or forsake you.
All things are possible with God.

PEOPLE LEAVING THE CHURCH

We really hope that everyone in the church loves us! However, do not be disillusioned if you find there is one or two or even more, that do not love you. It happens!

There are many reasons why people leave a church. With love and concern, you may ask them why they are leaving. Ask if there is something you can do to help them to work through the situation or problem.

Perhaps there has been some sort of misunderstanding. They may just need someone to encourage them and let them know that you care about what they may be going through.

There are other reasons why people leave the church.

Some need to go to a church closer to them; they may want to be with family members that are in another church; they may have doctrinal differences and convictions, and choose to find a church that shares their viewpoints. They are leaving in good standing.

The reverse of this is: Maybe there are those who say: they don't like the way the preacher preaches; or the song leader leads; they want to go somewhere they can be fed; they love to spread gossip; stir up confusion; create division; have a critical spirit; want their own way; or they continually create undercurrents. They may decide to leave the church and try to take others with them thus disrupting the unity of the church.

Through it all, as you pray, seeking God about how to handle the situation commit it to God for Him to work out. Follow close to God, preaching the truth with wisdom, love and compassion.

God may be working and does not need your help with the problem. God will either move them in, move them out, or He may allow them to remove themselves. *Sometimes it may be wise to let them go!*

NOTE: Use caution and wisdom when confronting or dealing with problems. The pulpit is not to be used as a whipping post or to a place to exert a get even spirit when and if you have been hurt.

It is best not to use the pulpit as an occasion to skin the sheep. Sheep can be sheered many times, but can only be skinned once.

GOING THROUGH THE FIRE

We were excited about becoming pastors of our first church. We looked forward to what God had in store for us as we entered the ministry on a full time basis. During our first year, new families were added to the congregation.

Several people were saved, and miracles of healing took place.

One lady had a very large cancerous growth on her leg. When she was prayed for that cancer dropped off her leg and she was completely healed. No more cancer!

The time for the annual business meeting was approaching. The first order of business was to cast a vote on the tenure of the present pastors, "us".

We were warned that this church had a reputation for causing their pastors to leave. That they had gone through seven pastors in ten years. Now, this is not what we needed to hear.

However, three families who were leaders in the church made it clear that they did not want us to continue as pastors. The other church members asked us to please stay with them because they were tired of their pastors being forced to leave.

As time for the meeting approached, it was like going through the fire for us. We continued praying for wisdom and guidance for our future, and for the future of that church.

Those three families were at work gathering everyone who had ever come to the church to attend that meeting and to cast their votes. They seemed determine to remove us as pastors.

Since we were young, and this was our first pastorate, we felt it would be using wisdom to invite the Sectional Presbyter to preside over the meeting so everything would be done properly.

He arrived early, and instructed my husband to make contact about the financial report. He was informed that there would be no report. The presbyter heard the conversation.

He asked for the church membership cards and went through them card by card, asking about each one. Had they been there the last three months, had they supported the church etc. He separated the cards with those active and qualified to vote, and those who were not.

When we entered the church, it was filled with people, many we had never seen or met. The Presbyter greeted the people and asked everyone to move out of the center section of the church, and proceeded to call the names of active members in good standing in the church.

As he called each name, he asked them to please move to the center section of the church. When he finished calling the roll, he invited those whose names were not called to remain as visitors however they would not be eligible to vote in the pastoral election or any other business to be discussed.

The meeting went well. We received all but the votes of the three families. We were elected as pastors for an indefinite term.

The following Sunday morning they were all present and filled their positions of: deacons, secretary treasurer, teachers, Sunday school superintendent and song leader. Each made statements of their resignations and left the church slamming the door.

We had prayed for unity in the church. God allowed them to remove themselves from the congregation. They became very bitter and continued to create problems for us, even though they were no longer in the church. We consistently showed Christian love which seemed to irritate them.

In those next months, it seemed that God dealt with them. Each family began experiencing devastating situations. The Scripture says,

> **Psalms 105:14-15, "He suffered no man to do them wrong: yea, He reproved kings for their sakes;"**

> **V15, "Saying, "Touch not Mine anointed, and do My prophets no harm."**

Through it all, we earnestly prayed that, if God was judging them that He would halt His judgments. One of the families return to the church and was a blessing. We pastored that church for over four years.

God blessed and the church grew from the seventeen in our first service, to ninety nine. To God, be all glory, honor and praise.

Sometimes church business meetings can be traumatic. I have shared this as a testimony that there are many ways to avoid conflicts and resolve problem situations.

REFRESHING AND RENEWING MY SPIRITUAL SELF

There are times when one experiences one stressful situation after the other. It seems like life is caving in on you, things are falling apart around you and your stress level is soaring out of control.

This sometimes happens when I allow myself to be surrounded by all the STUFFFF, or I get so busy that I neglect to keep my own personal time alone with God so my body, soul, spirit, and my mind is refreshed.

My motto is:

"Come apart and rest a while, before you come apart"!

It is a great motto, the only problem is, I sometimes forget to come apart and rest, (refresh and renew my spiritual self). That is when stress takes over, and I come apart.

Mark Chapters 5 and 6, The disciples were going through very stressful times. Their friend John the Baptist had been killed. They came to Jesus and told Him all they had been through. This is how He answered them.

> *Mark 6:31-32, "And He said unto them, "Come ye yourselves apart into a desert place, and rest a while:"*

for there were many coming and going, and they had no leisure so much as to eat."

V32, "And, they departed into a desert place by ship privately."

There are many situations that come into your everyday life. It is not always from church members. Sometimes it comes in your own household, and sometimes it is buffeting from Satan.

Sometimes, it would be well to count to ten before speaking, giving yourself time to evaluate the situation and decide your course of action, instead of unleashing your fury and later find it necessary to apologize for your actions.

In times like these, when the devil is buffeting you, especially if there seems to be conflict, and discord in the parsonage, or in the church, you may need to go through each room and tell the devil to get out. When you have gone through every room, open the door, and cast him out. Tell him this:

"Get out of this house Satan! This home, or this church, is the dwelling place of God, and there is no room or place for you. I command you to leave now. I take authority over you IN THE NAME OF JESUS!"

NOTE: *Then ask God to fill your home, or your church with His presence so there is not room, or place for the devil to reenter.*

We have experienced the powers of darkness trying to take over our home, our church and our lives.

This is spiritual warfare! On one occasion, we were awakened with such an evil presence in our home. We begin to "Plead the Blood of Jesus" over our lives, and our home. We went through the house room by room and in the Name of Jesus cast the evil influence and powers of darkness out of that room.

When we came to the door opened it and in the Name of Jesus commanded the evil and darkness to leave and shut the door. We asked God to fill our home with His presence, and His Holy Spirit.

When we did this, the darkness and oppression left our home. A peace that passes understanding came over us and our home was filled with the Glory of God. The Holy Spirit had taken control.

NOTE: *THE DEVIL IS REAL and he is powerful. He is desperate because his reign in the earth is coming to a close. He is going about seeking to destroy the minister, the family, the church and is responsible for the evil influence, turmoil and hate that is rampant in today's world.*

But know this: Satan cannot stand against the power of Almighty God and the anointing of the Holy Spirit in your life as a spirit filled believer and a child of God!

God is God and He always will be God. He will never lose His power. Jesus is our peace. Our peace comes from Him. Allow the Holy Spirit to sweep over your mind, body and spirit and speak peace in your time of need, as well as, when all is going well.

There are times when your faith and patience are tried to the "nth degree". That is when you must remember who you are in Christ Jesus.

We are the Called, the Chosen and the Commissioned by God Himself. He has given us a special anointing and authority to carry out that call that God placed on our life.

When you remember who you are in Him, you can cope with, or deal with whatever problem, test or temptation you face. God has given us His anointing, power, a sound mind and the authority to overcome all the power of satanic warfare.

THROUGH THE YEARS

God brought us through many situations. Some were heart breaking, and some brought joy to our hearts. Through these incidents, God taught us to walk in faith, and He gave us the wisdom and grace to deal with each individual situation.

When going through trying times, know that you are not the only one going through hard places or hard times.

May I encourage you to read: **1 Peter Chapters 3 and 4?** There you will find great wisdom and comfort for every day of your life?

> *1 Peter 4:12-13, "Beloved , think it not strange concerning the fiery trial which is to try you, as though some strange thing happened unto you: "*
>
> *V 13, "But rejoice, in as much as ye are partakers of Christ's Sufferings; that, when His Glory shall be revealed, ye may be glad also with exceeding joy."*

NOTE: *Prayerfully seek God in each situation, for His will; His solution; His plan; His guidance, and what you should or should not do.*

There is a place by God, where He places you in the cleft of the rock, as He did when Moses asked God to,

"Show me Thy Glory."

> *Exodus 33:18, "And he said, "I beseech Thee, show me Thy Glory."*
>
> *Exodus 33:21-22, "And the Lord said, "Behold, there is a place by Me, and thou shalt stand upon a rock:"*

V22, "And it shall come to pass, while My Glory passeth by, that I will put thee in a Clift of the Rock, and will cover thee with My Hand while I pass by."

NOTE: God said: *"There is a place by Me". And He will show us His Glory, just as He did for Moses.*

When you call on the Lord, He will hear and answer your call. God's phone number is,

> *Jeremiah 33:3, is "Call unto Me, and I will answer thee, and shew thee great and mighty things, which thou knowest not."*

I would not attempt to tell you that there is the only one way to deal with problems. The message here is that when you have a problem, you should call on the Lord, and,

NOTE: *He will show up, He will show His glory and He will take you through your every storm.*

*Know that God will take care of you when you are in that "**THERE PLACE"** where He has called you and chosen for you to minister.*

Through the years of ministry, we learned:
To trust God;
To live by faith;
To take Him at His word;
That He would do what He said He would do.
He would take care of us, as we walked daily with Him.

Know that when you are called by God to *"GO"*: You can be assured that He is saying:

"GO, AND I WILL BE WITH YOU THERE"!

"THERE" *Is that place I have called you to minister*
"THERE" *Is where I will be and where I will meet you*
"THERE" *Is where I have made provisions for you*

REWARDS OF BEING "THE PREACHER'S WIFE"

A young man began attending our church. Soon after this he was saved and received the Baptism into the Holy Spirit with the evidence of speaking in other tongues. The Lord spoke to us as pastors, that God had a call on his life, and that we should teach and guide him.

We watched him grow and mature in Jesus. He met this beautiful young Christian lady at a Youth Convention and soon they were married.

The next year, at Youth Convention, I saw them weeping together at the altar. The Lord let me know that, He was calling them into the ministry that very night!

When they got up from the altar they came straight to me. They were beaming. They told me they wanted me to be the first to know that God had just called them into the ministry. What an honor!

We hugged each other and wept as the joy of the Lord filled our hearts. We prayed together that God would anoint, lead and guide their every step as they accepted His call on their lives.

I watch their lives, as they fulfill that call as God leads and guides them. What a delight to have had a small part in God fulfilling His plan for their lives.

This is one of the most precious benefits of being:

The Preacher's Wife and A Woman in Ministry

Chapter 7

MY HOUSE SHALL BE CALLED "A HOUSE OF HOSPITALITY"

WHAT IS A HOUSE OF HOSPITALITY?

Hospitality is: A generous and friendly treatment of visitors and guests in a warm friendly way. It is the relationship between guest and host or the reception and entertainment of guests, visitors, and strangers, and the generous providing of care and kindness to whoever is in need and enters its door.

AS THE WIFE OF A MINISTER

When my husband was being interviewed for credentials, many of the questions were about the preacher's wife, "Me" I was asked:

"As the wife of a minister, do you consistently maintain a home that you would not be embarrassed or ashamed to have any of us, or members of the congregation to enter at *any time*?"

Now I ask you,

"As a Preacher's Wife, or A Woman in Ministry, could you say "YES" to this question?"

This question really scared me. I prayed and asked God to give me wisdom and the ability to live up to their expectations.

As I prayed, I thought perhaps the question was not so much as to whether or not my house was always spotless, and everything in its place, as much as it was about how people would feel when they came into our home.

Questions like:

Did they feel welcome?

Did they look forward to coming, when invited to our home?

Did they dread to come because the atmosphere was strained?

From that time forward, I would not go to bed at night until everything was clean, polished, and in its place. A neat and clean house is important,

NOTE: *What they wanted me to understand was the importance of making people feel welcomed, wanted, and comfortable when they entered our home.*

I recall, when I was just a small child, several important ladies came to our house. My mother was embarrassed because we had no furniture, only pallets on the floor, and an orange crate for our table. Mom apologized that there was no nice place for them to sit. This statement of one of the ladies has inspired me through the years. She said,

"We have been in beautiful houses that were well furnished but the atmosphere was cold and indifferent, they were just beautiful houses. Mrs. Palmer, you have a beautiful, happy home. There is a difference! There is warmth and love and a welcome here."

IS THE WELCOME MAT OUT AT YOUR HOME?

Through the years, our home has been a haven for hurting people, and some who just needed a place. There were teenagers, two foster boys, homeless and broken families, family members, singers, preachers, evangelists and missionaries and yes even sinners.

It has always been a place for family and friends to gather. We sometimes have over thirty people with us all through the holiday season.

There may be occasions when situations develop causing concern for your home and family. Times when those who enter or dwell in your home take advantage, create discord and upset the function, peace and tranquility of your home.

You are the protector of the sanctity, security, safety, and peace of mind for your home and family. Prayerfully seek God for wisdom and guidance as to how you should handle those times and situations.

There were times when our child was affected by our hospitality. This may seem small unimportant but it was my responsibility to consider her feelings and to protect her.

When some families came, their children would go into Debbie's room, pull out all of her toys and leave her to pick them up by herself. I saw that she was beginning to dread when those families came. We had a talk about the situation and I promised her I would take care of it on her behalf.

I did not want anything we did, to cause her to become bitter about her life as a preacher's kid.

After that, when those families came to our home, and they were about to leave, I went into Debbie's room, and told the children it was time for them to help Debbie pick up all the toys and put them away.

When all the toys were in their place, I thanked them for being such good helpers and good friends and invited them to come and play again. Problem solved...

OUR MISSION OF HOSPITALITY

Our mission of hospitality is to make a difference in the lives of those God places in our path and in our home. Helping them to feel comfortable, and encouraged when in our presence and feeling good about themselves when they leave us, is part of our ministry of Hospitality.

There were times when their children ran wild in the parsonage. On these occasions, some of my special treasures were broken. After experiencing some of these situations, I made sure that no one would hate to see me come and bring my child into their home. I taught Debbie manners and respect for other people's things.

She knew she was to help pick up toys, and not to touch curios, etc. Usually she sat beside me or her daddy, unless there were children for her to play with.

ENTERTAINING GOD'S CHOSEN

Many times we have taken someone in, who was a great blessing to us. I am thinking of one occasion at a General Council meeting held in a large convention center. A lady, who was in her late eighties, took hold of my arm. She was very upset, and through her tears she cried,

"What am I going to do? Oh! What am I going to do?"

I asked her to tell me what I could do to help her.

She told me that her people did not come to pick her up and take her home after the service. That she lived in another town several miles away. She had no money, and no place to spend the night. Now, you can't spend the night in a convention center auditorium.

Debbie and I realized that she was in a desperate situation. I told her not to worry. She could spend the night with us, and in the morning we would make contact with her friends and everything would be alright for her.

We had never seen her before. It had to be God who brought her to us out of the thousands of people at that convention center auditorium.

We took her out to eat, then to our hotel room to spend the night. All night, she talked of her experiences as a Missionary to China in the early days when Communism took over the country.

She was one of our great pioneer missionaries who many times had risked her life and had gone through so much for the cause of Christ. What a blessing she was to us. Our lives were so enriched because God allowed us to meet her.

Another time, a group of Gospel Singers, were invited to a youth rally to sing. However, it was a Speed the Light Rally. All the offerings were designated for that ministry. This meant that the singers did not receive any offering. They needed a place to spend the night so we invited them to stay at our house. What a night, we had a house full, four people slept on two twin size bunk beds.

The next morning the singers asked me to travel with them to play the piano. I told them I had married a husband who was a preacher, and I was the preacher's wife, so I could not go. My life has been so blessed and enriched. Things are always exciting at the parsonage.

God has permitted me to entertain so many of His ministers,

missionaries, Gospel singers, preacher's families and His people in "My Home of Hospitality".

Whether it was in my home, my hotel room, or wherever God chose to bring someone to us, we ministered to them. Many times, they were the ones who ministered to us.

Just a tip: When entertaining missionaries in your home, if at all possible find out if they have need of special diets or special accommodations so you can prepare accordingly.

I recall entertaining one of our great pioneer missionaries in our home. He was very kind, and hesitated to inform us of his need for a special diet, and certain physical requirements. If we had known in advance, we could have prepared adequate provisions for his comfort. We quickly responded, and all went well.

One can relax and enjoy your guests when being prepared to accommodate and make their stay pleasant and enjoyable. Thank You, Lord for bringing these special people into our lives.

EXPRESSING APPRECIATION

My Mother taught us to be respectful of others, of their feelings, and their possessions. We were to express appreciation when someone did something for us, or gave us a gift, whether it was great or small.

Most of all, she taught us to say _"Please"_ if we asked for something and to say _"Thank You"_ when we received what we asked for, and that,

"Please and Thank You" are model words expressing respect and appreciation.

When anyone brought a gift, or did something special for us we made sure we expressed appreciation and thanked them for their kindness to us.

THREE CHOCOLATE PIES

When we arrived at our first church to begin as pastors, a lady in the church made three chocolate pies and brought them to the parsonage for us. They were delicious. We thanked her and let her know how much we appreciated her labor of love, and what a blessing she was to us. We would always ask the Lord to bless her for her ministry to us.

This lady became ill and was unable to care for her family, yet she never missed a Saturday in four years making and sending three chocolate pies to the parsonage for her pastor's family. Even when they were not eatable we made sure she knew how much we appreciated her faithful ministry.

When people know you appreciate what they do for you they enjoy ministering to you. Expressing appreciation for everything, small or great is pleasing to the Lord. I trust you remember to give thanks to God for His blessings to you as well.

THE WORLD WE LIVE IN TODAY

There is a general attitude we see in this generation of children and adults of not being thankful or appreciative for things they have and things they receive. They seem to think that the world owes them and they expect everyone to give them what they want.

It is sad when such attitudes try to invade our churches.

If there are those who stir discord or cause problems, we are given instructions to mark those attitudes and spirits in "Jesus Name" when we pray.

Romans 16:17-18, "Now I beseech you, brethren mark them which cause divisions and offenses contrary to the doctrine which ye have learned; and avoid them."

V18, "For they that are such serve not our Lord Jesus Christ, but their own belly; and by good words and fair speeches deceive the hearts of the simple."

He has called us to lead and build His church.

He has given us a solid foundation, the keys to the kingdom and the authority to use them. The Bible says in:

Matthew 16:18-19, "And I say also unto thee, "That thou art Peter, and upon this rock I will build My church: and the gates of hell shall not prevail against it."

V19, "And I will give unto thee the keys of the kingdom of heaven: and whatsoever thou shalt bind on earth shall be bound in heaven: and whatsoever thou shalt loose on earth shall be loosed in heaven."

BATTLE FATIGUE

Adapted from and inspired by Reverend Patty (Hogan) Hughart and is used by permission.

Lately I have noted statements from ministers and minister's wives who have been in the ministry for any length of time that they are experiencing what I call "BATTLE FATIGUE". Some have been attacked physically with health problems, some with discouragement who have become weary with day by day problems and stresses. Some have even become weary in well doing, and in battling spiritual warfare.

Pastors and Pastor's Wives, help those who have suffered at the hands of others. This means they have gone into Satan's territory and come against him on behalf of those who have been abused. They have the battle scars to prove it. There comes a time when it takes its toll, because Satan has and is attacking continually with day to day problems and stresses.

We know that the Holy Spirit speaks in a still small voice into our ears and into our thoughts. At the same time, Satan also has a voice and whispers his poison in our ear and into our thoughts.

Unlike the still small voice of the Holy Spirit who speaks His peace and comfort to you, Satan tries to tear down your resistance and cause you to feel like you are a failure or mistreated and no one cares.

There are those with health problems. Satan tells you that there is no hope, that you will never be any better. Again and again he uses his voice in your ear to bring thoughts of fear and doubt, hopelessness and discouragement.

Then there are those who stir trouble by making up stories and spreading them around. It is called spreading rumors, or gossip. As children we used to say:

"Sticks and stones may break my bones but "WORDS" can never hurt me!"

NOT TRUE! Oh yes, sticks and stones can break your bones. You and I know that words spoken and taken the wrong way can cause misunderstandings. They can hurt and destroy ones reputation, ministry, and even one's life. This happens when we are already stressed, not feeling well, or from someone who seems to enjoy creating discord.

It is those "Little Things" that can cause battle scars. I have seen church splits over the smallest most foolish things. Like:

Where to put the flag pole,
Or what color the carpet should be,
Or should the pews be padded.
Or why does sister _____ get to play the piano more than I do?

After a while, dealing with all the "stuff" can cause battle fatigue. There are times when you may find yourself in one or all of these situations. Through the years, and even recently I have experienced various times of "BATTLE FATIGUE".

The question is: What do you do to refresh your strength, renew your mind, or how do you overcome **"BATTLE FATIGUE?"**

The answer is: "SHUT YOURSELF IN WITH GOD," go into your secret prayer closet, your special place of prayer and shut the door, shutting out noise, distractions and interruptions.

Be like Mary of old, as she set at Jesus feet. There to listen for Him to teach and minister to her. Waiting in His presence, and allowing Him to pour a fresh healing anointing into your mind, body, soul and spirit. You will find you are gaining new power to run in this race, and to overcome all the fiery darts of the devil. When you pray,

Matthew 6:6, "But thou, when thou prayest, enter into thy closet, when thou hast shut thy door, pray to thy Father which is in secret; and thy Father which seeth in secret shall reward thee openly."

Then go through your home praying for God's blessing and His presence to fill each room of your "House of Hospitality" so there is nothing that is contrary to God's will or His presence.

Ephesians 6:10-20, "Finally, my brethren, be strong in the Lord, and in the power of His might."

V11, "Put on the whole armor of God, that ye may be able to stand against the wiles of the devil."

V12, "For we wrestle not against flesh and blood, but against principalities, against powers, against the rulers of the darkness of this world, against spiritual wickedness in high places."

V13, "Wherefore, take unto you the whole armor of God, that ye may be able to withstand in the evil day, and having done all, to "STAND,"

V14, "STAND THEREFORE, having your loins girt about with truth, and having on the breastplate of righteousness;"

V15, "And your feet shod with the preparation of the gospel of peace;"

V16, "Above all, taking the shield of faith, wherewith ye shall be able to quench all the fiery darts of the wicked,"

V17, "And take the helmet of salvation, and the sword of the Spirit, which is the Word of God:"

V18, "Praying always with all prayer and supplication in the Spirit, and watching thereunto with all perseverance and supplication for all saints;"

V19, "And for me, that utterance may be given unto me, that I may open my mouth boldly, to make known the mystery of the Gospel."

V20, "For which I am an ambassador in bonds: that therein I may speak boldly, as I ought to speak."

INSPIRING VOLUNTEERS TO SERVE IN GOD'S HOUSE

Do you ever feel like no one wants to serve, or work in the church?

Do you ever have a problem inspiring individuals to assume positions of leadership in the house of God?

When positions such as teachers, workers, greeters etc, need to be filled: try presenting these as opportunities for ministry in God's house in a manner that will inspire members in the congregation to open their hearts and respond.

Then, make sure that each volunteer has information, instructions and adequate training for carrying out that particular ministry.

NOTE: The lack of adequate preparation, training and instructions is sometimes the reason people hesitate to make commitments to leadership.

A dedication ceremony for ALL the volunteers and workers is appropriate!

Recognize each and their position, and have the congregation pray over them for God's Holy Spirit to anoint them to fulfill those positions of ministry.

Always, let them know that their efforts and ministry is appreciated. When individuals know that they are appreciated, they will go the second mile to fulfill that commitment.

Whether in your home or in your church, Hospitality opens doors for ministries to fulfill God's commission to:

Reach the lost and to
Prepare His church for His Coming!

Chapter 8

FEAR, FAITH AND TRUST

LIVING UNDER GOD'S UMBRELLA

This chapter highlights the importance of recognizing that God is a very personal God. He is interested in and concerned about everything that affects our lives and the things we deal with in our everyday life.

It is as if He has placed His umbrella of loving care over us. So open your spiritual eyes to see, your ears to hear, your mouth to speak and see what God will do on your behalf.

In these last days many Christians are being overcome with fear because of all the events taking place in our world. When we have Jesus as our Lord and Savior, we have nothing to fear.

> *2 Timothy 1:7, "For God has not given us a spirit of fear; but of power, and of love, and of a sound mind."*

Throughout the scripture, God has made provision, given wisdom, and He has come to the aid of His people.

Those who have learned to trust Him are fully aware of His personal intervention and they experience a peace of mind and spirit.

Think about how God spoke to individuals giving instructions,

information, assurance and peace during their time of trouble. He will speak to you just as He did to those in the Bible.

SIMON PETER:
SATAN HAS DESIRED TO HAVE YOU

Luke 22:31-32, "And the Lord said, "Simon, Simon, behold, Satan hath desired to have you, that he may sift you as wheat:"

V32, "But I have prayed for thee, that thy faith fail not!"

Think about it: Simon Peter is not the only one that Satan desires to have that he may sift as wheat. Ever felt like you were sifted or weak in times of danger, fearful situations, trouble, or problems? Jesus said, to Simon Peter,

"I have prayed for you that your faith fail not!"

The Bible says that *(right now)* Jesus is at the right hand of the Father, making intercession on our behalf. He has given us His power, His love, and a sound mind to cope with, and to deal with whatever Satan hurls at us.

Romans 8:34-39, "Who is he that condemneth? It is Christ that died, yea rather, that is risen again, Who is even at the right hand of God, Who also maketh intercession for us."

V35, (Think about it): "Who shall separate us from the love of Christ? Shall tribulation, or distress, or persecution, or famine, or nakedness, or peril, or sword?"

V37, "Nay, in all these things we are more than conquerors through Him that loved us."

V38, "For I am persuaded, that neither death, nor life, nor angels, nor principalities, nor powers, nor things present, nor things to come,"

V39, "Nor height, nor depth, nor any other creature, shall be able to separate us from the love of God, which is in Christ Jesus our Lord."

I trust you will read these promises over and over until they get into your spirit. They are POWERFUL PROMISES given to us!

THE APOSTLE PAUL:
THE ANGEL OF GOD STOOD BY ME

Paul was a prisoner on a prison ship when a terrible storm arose that continued for fourteen days and nights. Paul speaks and encourages his shipmates.

Acts 27:22-25, "And now I exhort you to be of good cheer: for there shall be no loss of any man's life among you, but of the ship,"

Paul tells them how he knows this.

V23, "For there stood by me this night the angel of God, Whose I am, and Whom, I serve," (think about this!)

V24, "Saying "Fear not, Paul; Thou must be brought before Caesar: and, lo, God hath given thee all them that sail with thee."

V25, "Wherefore, sirs, be of good cheer: for I believe God that it shall be even as it was told me."

Have you ever been in a desperate situation and felt the angel of the

Lord standing beside you when you were fearful of which way to turn, or what to do?

They are shipwrecked, their ship has sunk, the storm is still raging, they are in the sea, fearing that they are about to drown, and *Paul tells them to be of good cheer*, that none of them is going to die!

And it was, just as the angel told Paul it would be. Not one life was lost. All reached the shore of the Island of Melita safely.

THE APOSTLE PAUL: SHAKE OFF THAT SNAKE

Acts 28: 3-6, "And when Paul had gathered a bundle of sticks, and laid them on the fire, there came a viper out of the heat, and fastened on his hand."

V4, "And when the barbarians saw the venomous beast hang on his hand, they said among themselves, "No doubt this man is a murderer, whom though he hath escaped the sea, yet vengeance suffereth not to live."

V5, "And he shook off the beast into the fire, and felt no harm."

V6, "Howbeit they looked when he should have swollen, or fallen down dead suddenly: but after they had looked a great while, and saw no harm come to him, they changed their minds, and said that he was a god."

On the Island of Melita, Paul gathered sticks and placed them on a fire, a poison viper fastened on his hand. Now, the others stood speechless, expecting him to die any second. *Paul had complete trust in God*. What did he do?

He shook that snake off his hand and into the fire. He did not experience any effects of the poison of that snake.

When Satan tries to put his stronghold bite on you,

SHAKE THAT SNAKE OFF YOUR HAND,

And continue to build up the Fire of God in your life: Trusting God in every situation.

Psalms 91:11, "For He shall give His angels charge over thee, to keep thee in all thy ways."

ELISHA AND HIS SERVANT: OPEN OUR SPIRITUAL EYES LORD

The King of Syria was at war with the King of Israel. Every time they went out against Israel, they were defeated. The King questioned his servants as to who was informing Israel of his secret plans. One said,

> *2 Kings, 6:12, "And one of his servants said, "None, my lord, O king: but Elisha, the prophet that is in Israel, telling the king of Israel the words that thou speakest in thy bedchamber."* (God was telling Elisha their secret plans)

So the King of Syria sent his army, horses and chariots by night to find Elisha and take him prisoner. They surround the city where Elisha and his servant were sleeping. When the servant woke up, he looked out and saw that the enemy had compassed the city, with horses and chariots. He said to Elisha,

> *2 Kings 6:15-20, ..."Alas, my master! How shall we do?"*

> *V16, "And he answered, "FEAR NOT: for they that be with*

> *us are more than they that be with them."*
>
> *V17, "And Elisha prayed, and said, "Lord, I pray Thee, open his eyes, that he may see." And the Lord opened the eyes of the young man; and he saw: <u>and, behold, the mountain was full of horses and chariots of fire round about Elisha."</u>*
>
> *V18, "And when they came down to him, Elisha prayed unto the Lord, and said, "<u>Smite this people I pray with blindness.</u>" And <u>He smote them with blindness according to the word of Elisha."</u>*
>
> *V19, "And Elisha said to them, "This is not the way, neither is this the city: follow me and I will bring you to the man whom you seek." But, he led them to Samaria."*

NOTE: *God has given us power, love, a sound mind and a measure of faith to trust Him and to deal with any fearful situation, and to overcome any of Satan's attempts to build up his stronghold in our lives.*

> *V20, "And it came to pass, when they were come into Samaria, Elisha said, "Lord, open the eyes of these men, that they may see." And the Lord opened their eyes, and they saw; and behold, they were in the midst of Samaria."*

They saw their enemy, the King of Israel. Elisha told the king not to kill these men, but to provide a meal for them, and send them back to the king of Syria in defeat.

NOTE: **We have this same authority.** *Remember the situation I shared earlier about the man who was threatening us, how strong he was, and how the Holy Spirit spoke through me and told him not to cross the threshold of our door and the Holy Spirit backed him off our porch and did not let him come back.*

This is the real world we are living in, and this is also the real power and anointing God has given us through the Holy Spirit. As the scripture says,

> 2 Timothy 1:7-14, "For God has not given us the spirit of fear; but of power, and of love, and of a sound mind."

> V8, "Be not thou therefore ashamed of the testimony of our Lord, nor of me His prisoner: <u>but be thou partaker of the afflictions of the Gospel according to the power of God;</u>"

> V9, "<u>Who hath saved us, and called us with an holy calling, not according to our works, but according to His own purpose and grace, which was given us in Christ Jesus before the world began,</u>"

> V10, "But is now made manifest by the appearing of our Savior Jesus Christ, who had abolished death, and hath brought life and immortality to light through the Gospel:"

> V11, "Where unto I am appointed a preacher, and an apostle and a teacher of the Gentiles."

> V12, "For the which cause I also suffer these things: nevertheless I am not ashamed: for <u>I know Whom I have believed, and am persuaded that He is able to keep that which I have committed unto Him against that day.</u>"

> V13, "Hold fast the form of sound words, which thou hast heard of me, in faith and love which is in Christ Jesus,"

> V14, "That good thing which was committed unto thee keep by the Holy Ghost which dwelleth in us."

NOTE: *We are prone to see the enemy, or the bad side of situations. We should be like this servant, and have our spiritual eyes opened, so we see that God has already prepared the way before us. He knows the end, from the beginning. He said in:*

> **Isaiah 65:24, <u>"And it shall come to pass, that before they call, I will answer; and while they are yet speaking, I will hear."</u>** *(Think about what this verse says!)*

NOTE: *When we call His name we have His undivided attention. God dispatches His angels to watch over us to keep us in all our ways.*

There are times when God allows us to be in places and situations we do not want to be in. These are times when we must pray and ask the Lord to open our spiritual eyes, and allow us to see His plan for us at this time.

PAUL AND SILAS: BEATEN, BRUISED AND IN PRISON

Paul and Silas had been beaten, and cast into prison. The jailer was charged to keep them safe. He immediately thrust them into the inner prison, and locked their feet in stocks.

Their wounds were hurting and their feet were numb. They chose to make the best of their situation. What did they do? Can you picture this?

> **Acts 16:25-36, "And at midnight Paul and Silas prayed, and sang praises unto God: and the prisoners heard them."**

Their worship reached the throne: God heard their prayers and praises and responded with an earthquake to set them free.

> **V26, "And suddenly there was a great earthquake, so**

that the foundations of the prison were shaken: and immediately all the doors were opened, and every one's bands were loosed."

V27. "And the keeper of the prison on awaking out of his sleep, and seeing the prison doors open; he drew his sword, and would have killed himself, supposing that the prisoners had been fled."

V 28, "But Paul cried with a loud voice, saying, "Do thyself no harm: for we are all still here." (Think about it, not one prisoner escaped from the prison) Imagine their thoughts!

V 29 "Then he called for a light, and sprang in, and came trembling, and fell down before Paul and Silas,"

V 30, "And brought them out, and said, <u>"Sirs, what must I do to be saved?"</u>

V 31, "And they said, "Believe on the Lord Jesus Christ and thou shalt be saved, and thy house."

V 32, "And they spake unto him the Word of the Lord, and to all that were in his house."

V 33, "And he took them the same hour of the night, and washed their stripes; and was baptized, he and all his, straightway."

V 34, "And when he had brought them into his house, he sat meat before them, and rejoiced, believing in God with all his house,"

The jailer and his whole family were saved and were baptized that night.

> *V 35, "And when it was day, the magistrates sent the serjeants, saying, "Let these men go."*

(God not only sent an earthquake and freed them He caused those who had imprisoned them to free them as well.)

> *V36, "And the keeper of the prison told this saying to Paul, "The magistrates have sent to let you go: and therefore depart, and go in peace."*

NOTE: *There are times when we find ourselves in places and situations where we do not want to be.*

Just as Paul and Silas definitely did not want to be in that prison, however, they recognized that God had a purpose for them to be in that situation at that particular time. The jailer and his whole family were saved.

Oh, it is God's plan that we live our daily lives as these: in complete faith and trust.

THE RIGHT PLACE AT THE RIGHT TIME

Let's bring it forward to our times today....

When my Dad was saved, He was delivered from drinking, smoking, and cursing. He was a new born again child of God. By faith he trusted God to take care of him and his family.

When he developed pneumonia my Mother feared for his life and took him to the hospital. He was very angry with her because he felt his testimony of healing would be damaged, for he did not even take an aspirin, he totally trusted God.

The Lord woke my Dad in the night and told him that,

"The man in the next bed is having a heart attack. That he was to get up and go to him, touch his arm and tell him that God loves him, that he will be alright. Then pray for him, ring for the nurse and get back into your bed."

Dad made his way to the man's bed and told him what God had said. He prayed for him, rang for the nurse and got back into bed. When the nurse came, they coded the man, and he became stable. Later that day, the man looked at Dad, and said,

"Mister, tell me about this God who woke you up and told you to get out of your bed and pray for me. I want to know Him. I could not ring for help. If you had not been here last night and prayed for me I would have died." Dad led that man to Jesus.

My Dad did not want to be there, until God opened his spiritual eyes and he realized that God had ordained that he should be there, in the middle of that night, to intercede on behalf of this man.

NOTE: *So, when and if you find yourself in a place or situation you do not want to be in, ask God if He has an assignment for you and what He would have you do!*

God has a plan and a purpose for everything He allows into your life. It may be to reveal something to you personally, other times it may be on behalf of someone else.

GOD INVADED MY DREAM

Many times I have been awakened to intercede for a particular person, or need, other times, to stand in the gap and make up the hedge.

God sometimes invades our thoughts and dreams. This particular dream was very real and very specific. I felt the urgency to intercede on behalf of those involved. It is as though God invaded my dream to alert me to an urgent need.

In my dream, I saw a church building that I had never seen before. A man was intense in what he was doing. He was setting fires all around this building intending to burn it down.

I recognized the family sleeping inside as my dear friends Terry and Nita Watkins and their children. They were missionaries in the Far North of Alaska, thousands of miles from Arkansas. In my dream, they were unaware of the danger.

I woke up in a cold sweat, feeling the urgency to intercede on their behalf. I prayed until I felt that God had indeed heard, and by faith I trusted God to protect this family.

The next day, I called my friends. I asked them if everything was okay. They told me that a man in the village had threatened their lives, and that they felt very uneasy about the situation.

I told them my dream, and the urgency I sensed and assured them that I would continue to intercede on their behalf.

I asked them for a picture of their church building. When I received the picture it was the very same building I had seen in my dream. This truly was a confirmation that God had indeed invaded my dream.

A few days later, my friend called and told me that the man who had threatened their lives, had left their village..

This man may never know why he left that village up on the Tundra in far North Alaska, but I know, it was because God intervened and moved him out on behalf of this family.

WHEN GOD INTERRUPTS, BE QUICK TO OBEY

God may prompt you to call someone and encourage them. Be sensitive to this invasion of your thoughts. He may have chosen you to minister to them and perhaps save their life.

STOP what you are doing and make the call. That person may be desperate and need immediate help. They may have said,

"God, if you are real, if you really care about me have someone call me right now, or else......."

God has equipped us with the Holy Spirit so we can recognize when He is invading our dreams or when He interrupts our thoughts and be quick to respond. He has given to every man and woman a measure of faith to trust Him in every situation.

> *Isaiah 12:2-6, "Behold, God is my salvation; I will trust, and not be afraid: for the Lord Jehovah is my strength and my song; He also is become my salvation."*
>
> *V3, "Therefore with joy shall ye draw water out of the Wells of Salvation."*
>
> *V4, "And in that day shall ye say, "Praise the Lord," call upon His Name, declare His doings among the people, make mention that His Name is exalted."*
>
> *V5, "Sing unto the Lord; for He hath done excellent things: that is known in all the earth."*
>
> *V6, "Cry out and shout, thou inhabitant of Zion: for great is the Holy One of Israel in the midst of thee."*

**WHEN FEAR COMES,
FAITH AND TRUST IN GOD
TAKES OVER!**

Chapter 9

WORDS OF WISDOM

BY: PREACHER'S WIVES AND
WOMEN IN CHRISTIAN MINISTRY

Representing over seven hundred years of ministry. Each has written their testimonies for this book, that you may be encouraged, strengthen and blessed as you fulfill God's call on your life and ministry.

"ENJOY THE JOURNEY"
> By: Mrs. Johanna Garrison

"THE JOYS OF BEING CALLED"
> By: Reverend Martha Tennison

"HELPFUL HINTS FOR HAPPY LIVING FOR MY SOUL SISTERS"
> By: Reverend Judy Moore

"AN ARRANGED MARRIAGE"
> By: Reverend Debbie Young

"BEARING FRUIT"
> By: Reverend Debbie Young

"THE WIFE OF THE PREACHER"
> By: Reverend Stephanie Hodges

"GET A WHIFF OF THAT AROMA"
  By: Reverend Patty Hogan Hughart

"GET RID OF THAT POISON"
  By: Reverend Patty Hogan Hughart

"MY JOURNEY THROUGH GRIEF"
  By: Reverend Teena Whaley Culbreth

"A DOZEN ROTTEN EGGS"
  By: Reverend Peggy Caldwell

"TEACH YOUR CHILDREN DILIGENTLY"
  By: Reverend Trudy Jackson

"WHAT I WANT TO BE!"
  By: Miss. Shirleyna Jackson

"EXPERIENCE OF A PASTOR'S WIFE"
  By: Reverend Wanda Huie

"FEELING INADEQUATE"
  By: Reverend Pam Johnson

"LIFE IS ONLY AS GOOD AS YOUR MIND SET"
  By: Reverend Jane Powell Carpenter

"STEP BY STEP, I KEPT MY VOW"
  By: Reverend Nadine Waldrop

"IT'S A GREAT LIFE BEING THE PREACHER'S WIFE"
  By: Mrs. Barbara Blann

"BACK TO BASICS, WE WIN"
  By: Reverend Angelia Carpenter

"ENJOY THE JOURNEY"

By: Mrs. Johanna Garrison

Johanna and her husband, Doctor Alton Garrison ministered as evangelists for nine years, later they served as team pastors at First Assembly of God in North Little Rock, Arkansas. When her husband served as the Arkansas District Superintendent of the Assemblies of God, she mentored minister's wives. Her ministry changed again when he served as the Assistant General Superintendent of the Assemblies of God. Her book "Tangled Destinies" is an account of her family's hardships through the Holocaust. I trust you will note how her role continued to change and how she prepared herself for each phase of ministry.

"ENJOYING MY JOURNEY"

My husband was an evangelist when we married. I served alongside him in that role for nine years.

Neither he nor I envisioned pastoral ministry, but when it materialized I was excited. I also wanted to prepare myself for the peaks and valleys that might come, as many voices were discouraging and giving warnings of the struggles of being a "Pastor's Wife."

I was unprepared and needed help and resources. I knew one of the fastest ways for me to obtain wisdom was to seek mentors. I developed relationships with some mentors.

And others taught me from afar through books and conferences. From them, I received candid, realistic, helpful, affirming, and godly advice. Their seasoned insights and encouragement helped me avoid mistakes and pitfalls as well as navigating as a leader.

A Woman in Ministry, and a Pastor's Wife
"ENJOY THE JOURNEY"

Mrs. Johanna Garrison

"THE JOYS OF BEING CALLED"

By: Reverend Martha Tennison

Martha and her husband Reverend Don Tennison are ordained ministers in the Assemblies of God. They have pastored, and evangelized across the country. She has ministered many times at Arkansas District Women's Retreats and preached in most of our churches. She is known and loved for her humor, her stories and most of all for anointed preaching of God's Word. This is her testimony of her Joy as a preacher's wife. Recently Brother Tennison finished his course, kept his faith, and entered his heavenly home.

"Keeping My Priorities"

I formally accepted the call to become a pastor's wife on June 6, 1970, the day I married Reverend Don Tennison. On that day, I became a pastor's wife but I knew before I said my marriage vows that my commitment to marriage also involved a commitment to ministry.

When I publicly promised to be a faithful and loving wife, I was also promising to partner with my husband as we served the Lord together.

After over forty-nine years of marriage together, including pastorates at three different churches, I can honestly say that the opportunity to serve God as a companion of the shepherd to God's people has been one of the greatest joys of my life.

From the beginning, I had to take steps to ensure that serving as a pastor's wife remained a joy. It is important that we keep a balanced life. We are first a child of God, then a companion to the pastor, a parent to our children, and then a leader in our church.

My first priority was not to be so busy working for God that I forgot to enjoy Him.

Ministry must flow out of the relationship that we have with God, and not the other way around. Too many ministers, including pastor's wives, base their relationship with God on their ministry so that we are pastor's or pastor's wife first.

I had to keep my life with God the priority in prayer, Bible reading, etc, because God and not ministry was the center of my life.

If, I could not live life as a disciple of Jesus, then I would be in no position to help disciple others. I must make sure my walk with Him is valid, before I can serve my husband, minister to my child, and be a blessing to the church successfully.

My second priority was to keep the needs of my marriage and my family a priority over the needs of our church body.

Being a pastor's wife meant first being a good wife to the pastor. That also meant I was to serve my husband and not to use my husband's position to my ends.

The call to serve as a companion to the pastor involves teamwork. We don't *compete* with each other, but we *complete* one another. I had to help wherever I could, and I needed to remain an encouragement to him at all times.

Ministry can be discouraging, and I am sure there were times my husband was more an encouragement to me, then I was to him.

When I became a mother, my priorities shifted again. Being a wife and mother was God's calling to me just as much as serving the church, and my husband and son needed me more than the church did.

The church could have many pastors and pastor's wives over the years, but my husband was only going to have one wife, and my son only one mother.

I did not always keep that priority where it should have been, because difficult times in the life of our church members sometimes called for extra love and attention to the church. However, I could not maintain my joy in serving the church if my family suffered because of it.

My third priority was to remember the needs of the church were a priority over the needs of my own ego.

I had to find my satisfaction in God, because I could not turn to the church to meet a need that only God can fill.

Sometimes we pour our heart and soul into a community, and the cost will not seem worth it if we are looking to the church to pay that bill.

We become discouraged because of the indifference of some and the unfaithfulness of others. We must remember we are not rewarded because of results, but because of our obedience. When we are faithful to God, then He is faithful with results. God is a great bookkeeper.

We need to serve the Lord with all our soul, mind, and strength because God has done more than we could ever repay. God has blessed me with a wonderful husband and the opportunity to serve Him in the ministry.

That ministry has remained a JOY IN MY LIFE, but only because I kept my priorities in place. The Church will not sustain your marriage, your family, or your relationship with God. God sustains the rest, and God must remain your priority. For:

THE JOY OF THE LORD,
IS MY STRENGTH.

Reverend Martha Tennison

"HELPFUL HINTS FOR HAPPY LIVING FOR MY SOUL SISTERS"

By: Reverend Judy Moore

Judy, and her husband Reverend Larry Moore have ministered together for many years. She is a Mom of two children and Nane of four grands; a licensed minister for fifteen years. and a Dental Hygienist R.D.H.B.A. with River Valley Pediatric Clinic. When they pastored First Assembly of God Church in Russellville, Arkansas she served as Children's Pastor and Evangelist for twelve years. Brother Moore is the Arkansas District Superintendent of the Assemblies of God, and Judy serves as the Arkansas District Women's Ministries Director and Coordinator of the Arkansas Leading Ladies.

"MY HELPFUL HINTS: FOR HAPPY LIVING FOR MY SOUL SISTERS"

My thoughts and advice for you my Soul Sisters, is to always be "YOUR SELF" Here are some helpful hints for happy living as they came to mind, to help along your way.

1. Be yourself
2. Pray hard
3. Love your husband and kids
4. Love people.
5. Give a lot of time, talents and money
6. Sow seeds and watch God work miracles for you.
7. Clean house
8. Save money
9. Lose weight
10. Exercise, go to the gym
11. You are an example
12. Eat healthy

13. God heals but He expects you to do your part to stay healthy
14. Faith without works is dead.
15. OK, you are "Chosen" picked out by God with a special purpose and assignment
16. The call: Go forward with God's direction.
17. You are the wife of a minister, or a pastor yourself, embrace.
18. Multi task
19. Always ask for help. You are not the "LONE RANGER".
20. The more people you ask to get involved, the more they will buy into your project
21. Get organized, be organized
22. Bind the devil, release the anointing
23. Get divine direction.
24. Be real
25. The "YOU" you see, is the "YOU" you'll be!
26. Pray for divine wisdom.
27. I would like to suggest a small book by Dr Cindy Trimm "Commanding Your Morning"
28. Decree, declare and command your day.
29. You have the "POWER" and "AUTHORITY", "USE IT"!
30. The Lord Almighty will walk with you through the fire.

"I HAVE BEEN THERE"!
LIVE LIFE TO THE MAX!
MAKE THE JOURNEY FUN!!
BE BLESSED AND
BE BALANCED!

Reverend Judy Moore

"AN ARRANGED MARRIAGE"

By: Reverend Debbie Young

Debbie was saved as a teenager, and later was called into the ministry. She is an Ordained Assemblies of God Minister. She directed the Missionettes Program in her church, for nineteen years, and served as a Sectional Missionettes Rep for six years. One of her students was our first Down's Syndrome girl to be crowned an Honor Star. She and her husband Glen served as the Children's Pastor, which included a bus ministry, at Pottsville Assembly of God Church for sixteen years. They have organized and directed camps for children in Foster Care through the Royal Family Kids Organization for over twelve years. She has written two books: "REALMS OF GLORY". The testimony of how God has led and directed her life and ministry; and "THERE IS A RIVER", the coming end time revival. Available from her, A must read!

"GOD ARRANGED OUR MARRIAGE."

It takes a very special man of God to support his wife who is called into the ministry, feeling, that he has not been called, but understands that he has been chosen. I am married to such a man.

I tell people that ours was an "Arranged Marriage.

I asked God to allow me to meet the man that He picked out for me. One week after I prayed that prayer, God arranged for me to meet Glen.

God sometimes works in mysterious ways. As a favor to a friend, I agreed to go on a blind date. It was to be one date, and that was to be the end of it. At that time, Glen was not saved.

I spent the entire evening sharing Jesus with him. He seemed very interested so we continued to date. Our dates consisted of going to church and visiting revivals in the area. Glen was saved shortly after we met.

I do not recommend "missionary dating" but in this case, God was leading and working His will for us. We grew closer to each other, and most of all we drew closer to Jesus. We have been married for forty-one years as I write our story.

I have never heard him raise his voice, say an unkind word, or do anything ungodly. He has been a wonderful father and a good provider. He is the man of my dreams. I thank God for arranging my marriage.

I had a powerful experience with God when I was twenty-one. I knew without a doubt that I was called into the ministry. Glen accepted this, and was very supportive of this and for many years we worked together wherever God called us.

I had a part time job, and Glen worked full time. We taught Sunday school, Missionettes, Royal Rangers, Youth, and I got to preach occasionally.

In 1998 I felt the Lord calling me into full-time ministry. I was working thirty-two hours a week at a dentist office, and did not think I could work and commit to conduct Children's Crusades as well. We discussed this, and Glen allowed me to set a date to quit my job, but I felt that, deep down he really did not want me too.

We spent the next several months while I was still working, building our puppet stage, collecting music, puppets and sound equipment, getting ready for the date we had set to launch our crusade ministry.

Finally, time came for me to resign my position at the dentist's office. We had a few invitations on the calendar.

I respected him as head of the house. I knew we needed a truck to carry our equipment, so I prayed that the Lord would show Glen that we needed a truck. I tried not to do much in the way of buying things that we didn't need.

All the while I prayed that God would soften Glen's heart to be glad that I was called into full time ministry. God touched his heart and Glen allowed it, and I had his blessing, but I could tell he was not passionate about it yet. I knew that it had to come from God, not from me.

Almost a year went by after I quit my job to go into "full time ministry". I was concerned that I was definitely *not ministering full time*.

One day, I received a call to come and have lunch with someone. When I arrived, they told me to sit down and then they told me that they were going to cash in a CD and give us the money, so we could use it to pay off our house.

I was overwhelmed! As I drove home I heard the Lord speak to my heart saying that the person would deposit the money into our account on the very day of the one year anniversary of the date I had quit my job. That it would be more than the amount I would have made at that job in the entire year! Sure enough, that is exactly what happened!

Words can't express what a confirmation that was to my precious husband! We paid off our house. We got a truck, and the invitations for ministry started coming our way.

Glen would work all day, at his job and then we would pile into the truck, loaded with props, and head down the road to fulfill God's call. Glen would help set up equipment, operate the sound and the computer each night. I honestly think he was more excited about doing the crusades than I was.

Not long after this, the invitation came for me to come on staff as "full-time Children's Pastor at a local church. Glen has been there in every single service for sixteen years, working behind the scenes, making sure everything ran smoothly. Glen and I make a great team, working side by side. If I get an idea, and draw it on paper, he can build it.

He is so happy to support me in our ministry. In fact, he may say that he is not called into the ministry, but I think God has given him the ministry of helps and support.

There are many areas of ministry besides preaching. There are those who are chosen to be supporters, and to stand alongside. I cannot imagine doing all this without him!

God opened the door for us to receive training on how to conduct a camp for foster children. Glen was there with me all the way. He helped establish our camp, and has been a key factor for its success for the past twelve years.

When I get weary of all the responsibility of being the camp director, he is right there in my corner cheering me on. He is my biggest encourager.

I think the key has been to move slowly, and gently, allowing God to speak to Glen's heart, instead of me trying to cram it down his throat.

I honor him as the head of the house and he honors me, allowing me to fulfill the calling that I have on my life. He backs me one hundred percent.

When I am invited to preach in a church, I always ask Glen to stand and pray at the beginning of my message. He is my covering. It is so easy for me to submit to him.

God is the giver of good gifts, and one of my best gifts is my

"ONE IN A MILLION PRECIOUS HUSBAND"
THANK YOU GOD,
FOR ARRANGING OUR MARRIAGE

Reverend Debbie Young

"BEARING FRUIT"

By: Reverend Debbie Young

Psalms 1:3, "And he shall be like a tree planted by the rivers of water, that bringeth forth his fruit in his season; his leaf also shall not whither; and whatsoever he doeth shall prosper."

"Bringing Forth Fruit"

What happens when you transplant a fruit tree? Can you expect it to bear fruit that year? What about the next year, or the next? Many times it takes a few years for that tree to get established in its new location before it will begin to yield fruit again.

What if your tree finally begins to bear fruit but you decide that you did not want it there after all. So, you dig it up and move it again. You can certainly expect it to be a few more years before it will yield its fruit. If that happens too many times, it might cease from bearing fruit permanently.

There are many occasions in the teachings of Christ where He admonishes us to be fruitful, that is, to be a soul winner; and a disciple maker. Many times God plants us in a location. Things don't go as well as planned and the temptation arises to uproot and be re-located. If we can ride out the storm, so to speak, and stay planted, chances are we will find ourselves and our ministry being quite fruitful.

If you keep moving from church to church, chances are you will never be as fruitful for the Kingdom of God as you could be. Let yourself be established, rooted and grounded. Stay put and see just what might happen!

Psalms 1:3, "And he shall be like a tree planted by the rivers of water, that bringeth forth his fruit in his season; his leaf also shall not wither, and whatsoever he doeth shall prosper."

Reverend Debbie Young

"THE WIFE OF THE PREACHER"

By: Reverend Stephanie Hodges

Stephanie became a preacher's wife when she married Reverend Matthew Hodges who served as Youth Pastor in her home church. They continued in that position for another year. They were invited to serve as senior pastors in another church, and became new parents for the first time. Eleven years later, they now have three beautiful children. She serves alongside her husband as Senior Pastors at First Assembly of God Church in Wynne, Arkansas.

"MY GREATEST CHALLENGES"

The greatest challenges I face as a Pastor's Wife is fulfilling my role as The Pastor's Wife to the church, and that of a Wife to my Husband and a Mother to My Children.

Family time has perhaps come more easily for us than other ministry families, because of my husband's commitment to spending time with his family outside of the church and its activities.

My greatest challenge to date is my relationship with my husband where the church is concerned. Yes, he is the Pastor, and yes, I am his wife,

QUESTION: But where does the role of pastor and pastor's wife become just man and wife again?

I am afraid that many marriages have no place to express themselves apart from the couple's role at the church. It has been one of our greatest struggles.

The church places many expectations on the two of us. Some we are confident in meeting. Others we are completely inadequate to fulfill.

My husband has released me, and more importantly I have released myself, to just be Mom and Wife.

My husband however is on call at every moment. He may be called from dinner, from a date, from a family outing, etc. He especially is pulled in so many directions concerning any given church issue.

That his only solace is in retreat to a quiet, neutral place, free from these opinions and expectations. My inclination is to love him, encourage him and in the next breath to become one of these voices, incessantly pressing him for the sake of what I perceive to be right! In his frustration, I see the expectations that I have placed on him.

In a moment of passionate debate in which I am desperately trying to convince him of my own perspective of a matter. I realize that he is surrounded on ALL sides. In these moments there is no place of retreat for him.

I have made it my number one goal in our marriage to provide a place of retreat for him in our home. Home needs to be more than a *"glorified break room"*. It needs to be a place of unconditional acceptance, full of love and affirmation. I'm a huge work in progress on the subject.

Yes, I have my opinions and at times, I will still share them when I think it is beneficial. But mostly I will pray for him, and trust not only him, but God who has called him.

I will trust the Lord to grant him wisdom beyond his years because I have asked Him for it.

I will trust my husband to be the man of God that I know him to be, and

I will not take the responsibility for decisions that are not mine to make in the first place.

Reverend Stephanie Hodges

"GET A WHIFF OF THAT AROMA"

By: Reverend Patty Hogan Hughart

Patty grew up as a (PK) preacher's kid. She began her ministry at age sixteen as a Sunday school teacher. She was a youth president, music pastor, wrote and directed dramas, some at Arkansas Women's Retreats, others in churches and in prisons. She and her husband Reverend Bill Hughart are Ordained Assemblies of God Ministers and have evangelized, conducted kids crusades, and served in pastoral ministry for "50" years. She was the Assistant Arkansas District Women's Ministries Director for ten years. Presently they serve as Associate Pastors of Pastoral Care for Senior Adults at First Assembly of God Church in Searcy, Arkansas. Used by permission.

"A CHRIST-LIKE AROMA"

2 Corinthians 2:15 "Our lives are a Christ-like fragrance rising up to God." (NLT)

I have a friend, who is a beautiful well dressed lady. But the thing that is so interesting is, as she passes by there is a lovely fragrance that is extremely pleasing. I may not even know that she is anywhere near, but when I get a whiff of that sweet-smelling perfume I look to see if she is nearby.

There are many minister's wives who feel that there is nothing they can do to help their husbands in the ministry, or to serve God.

Perhaps you can't play the piano, organ, or keyboard. Maybe God didn't bless you with a melodious voice so you can sing solos or sing in the choir. Possibly, you are not gifted with a teaching ministry. If so, you may feel like a failure.

Regardless of what you can or cannot do in the church services,

There is something that God desires for every Christian and especially every minister's wife to do.

He wants you to live so close to Him that there is a sweet smelling aroma that comes forth from your life so everyone that comes near you will know that you have been with Jesus.

It is so precious when we see a child try to imitate their parents in word, deed, or actions. It is also special when we, the children of God, attempt to imitate God. The Apostle Paul tells us in:

> *Ephesians 5:1-2, "Imitate God, therefore in everything you do, because you are His dear children." (NLT,)*

> *V2, "Live a life filled with love, following the example of Christ. He loved us, and offered Himself as a sacrifice for us, a pleasing aroma to God." (NLT,)*

Christ loved us so much that He offered Himself as a sacrifice that we may have eternal life. Therefore you should imitate Christ by living a self-sacrificing-life of love for others. Your love for others should cause you to pray for, witness to, and help people anyway you can so they can smell the fragrance of Christ coming forth from your life.

All Christians should exude a pleasing aroma from their lives that will attract others to Jesus Christ.

> *2 Corinthians 2:15, "Our lives are a Christ-like fragrance rising up to God." (NLT)*

Minister's wives are to be like a sweet perfume whose fragrance others can't help noticing. If you remain true to Christ, His Spirit working in you will attract others to Christ.

**Stay close to Christ so others will
get a whiff of the sweet aroma of Christ
as you walk by.**

Reverend Patty Hogan Hughart

"GET RID OF THE POISON"

By: Reverend Patty Hogan Hughart

Used by permission.

"But if ye do not forgive, neither will your Father which is in heaven forgive your trespasses." (Mark 11:26)

"WHY MUST I FORGIVE?"

Many minister's wives have been hurt by some of the parishioners. They have forgiven them for the things they have said about them or their family members. However, many of the same people have continued to ridicule, or tell lies on them over and over again.

Many minister's wives have allowed bitterness to build up in their lives. Some are tired of constant battles they face. They just want out of the ministry.

The following is a true story, but I won't give names. Rumors have gone around about an individual. One group in the church believed the rumors were true; the other group said they weren't. All of the people involved became so angry that hatred filled their hearts.

A few years later, one of the ladies went to the hospital for a couple of days for tests... nothing serious. One afternoon a young nurse came into the room. The patient recognized that she was the daughter of one of the ladies she hated. She became angry and screamed,

"Get out of here! Get out of here!"

The nurse came running and the doctor was called to get there as quickly as possible. The doctor came and checked her over. As he talked to the lady who was furious and trembling all over, it didn't take him long to find out what the problem was. He told the patient,

"You almost had a stroke. Your anger is going to kill you, just because you won't forgive."

Ladies, let me ask you a question.

"Have you been hurt by someone intentionally or unintentionally?"

If you dwell on it, and fail to let it go, it will cause other sins to enter your life: anger, resentment and hatred. When you fail to forgive it is like poison which causes bitterness, unhappiness, depression and even health problems.

UN-forgiveness will also affect your spiritual life. It takes away your happiness, peace, joy and your relationship with God. Jesus gives us a startling warning about forgiveness; if, you refuse to forgive others God will also refuse to forgive you.

> *"But if ye do not forgive, neither will your Father which is in heaven forgive your trespasses." Mark 11:26.*

It is easy to ask God to forgive us, but it is difficult to grant forgiveness to others. Minister's wives, you must daily ask God to forgive your sins, and when you do, you must ask yourselves,

"Have I forgiven the people who have wronged me?"

Ladies, get rid of the poison caused by UN-forgiveness. God didn't call you and your husband to serve a church full of perfect Christians. They are people who need help to become more like Christ. Forgive those who have wronged you, and pray for them to become more like Christ, and great will be your reward in heaven.

**You must forgive to be forgiven. When you do,
Your joy and peace will be restored!**

Reverend Patty Hogan Hughart

"A JOURNEY THROUGH GRIEF"

By: Reverend Teena Whaley Culbreth

Teena and her husband Reverend Dennis Whaley ministered together for thirty-six years, until he was called to his heavenly home. She shares her heart about her journey through grief, trusting that it will minister to others as they journey through their grief. In God's providence, she met and married Reverend Cecil Culbreth, together they continue in ministry. Both are credentialed ministers in the Assemblies of God. Her husband serves as the Arkansas District Secretary and Missions Director.

"MY JOURNEY THROUGH GRIEF"

An overwhelming sense of foreboding enveloped me as I was jolted awake in the wee hours of morning, before the dawn started its descent into the inky darkness. Alarmed, I immediately phoned the number of my husband's private nurse in the intensive care unit at the hospital, where he had undergone open heart surgery two days previously.

She assured me he was stable, but it was impossible to shake the uneasiness that gripped me. The surgeon had optimistically given us an eighty-five to ninety percent assurance of full recovery and, we believed that he would be restored and continue ministering effectively as always.

He had just turned fifty-eight a month before and we had celebrated thirty-six years of marriage and ministry three days prior to the operation. It would only be later on that same day, as he coded twice and life began to ebb from his earthly body that the realization came that God was preparing me for all that would transpire mere hours from that wake up call.

As my daughter, Sara, and I stood next to the lifeless earthly body of the man we had both loved unconditionally. My mind went into hyper gear,

"How could my life ever be wonderful again without the partnership we shared in both marriage and ministry?"

My mind, whirling like a giant propeller at breakneck speed glimpsed vignettes of moments throughout that life together. As time moved steadily forward though the memories, so many of those precious treasures were blurred as moments became weeks, and weeks months, and month's years.

I so wanted my tears to wash away the film that dulled my recollection of every special moment that built the great love story, with our names as the leading man and woman.

It was a love story that would outlast silly immaturity's in early years, difficulties and victories all of us in ministry encounter, painful infertility issues, fear of loss during life-threatening cancer, painful decisions while caring for all four of our parents, and now, outlast even physical death of the temporary body.

Let me admit something right here. It isn't easy letting go of the past. Why is that? Easy enough to answer! It is because that loved one is in the past and we naturally want to be where they are. One might ask:

"What it is that I have learned through this inconceivable journey?"

The unequivocal truth is that I have learned a volume about MYSELF. Through the most challenging and painful trials that we face in this life, WHO WE ARE comes through loud and clear.

It is hard to face the myriad of imperfections that make up our life, but absolutely necessary in order to come through the fire and continue to be productive as a Christ follower.

There are so many things about ME that God was not surprised with. When I began to question Him on a daily basis after my husband died.

He knows me intimately and therefore He KNEW, without a doubt, that I would be a pistol!

He was not surprised or dismayed by me wanting to know WHY, over and over and over and over again.

My ordeal began with total shock, which turned into the most agonizing, all-consuming pain I have ever experienced: from there, acceptance most of the time anyway, that: I will never know the answers, but also recognizing that it's okay somehow.

God, in His sovereignty, knew the events of my life before I was even born, and the plan He has for my life. It was ME who doubted everything. I have been amazed at His intimate nearness and continual presence.

It is overwhelming to acknowledge that this great God has a wonderful path for me, when there is so much about me that shouts, "BLEMISHED, FAULTY, WEAK, INADEQUATE."

My prayer is that I continue to chisel away at those imperfections and follow God with fervor and zeal.

Many of you will experience this same situation one day. Others will most definitely be close to someone who will go through this dark valley. We, as Christians, must live with HOPE of eternal life.

If, we are unable to cope with our loss, those around us who have watched our life, will not see what it means to live with hope. It will discourage them and destroy our testimony.

This is not to say we pretend that everything is fine and that we aren't hurting. We can be transparent in our grief and yet LIVE LIFE WITH HOPE.

That is the great gift we have in Jesus, hope that our loved one is in our future. Encourage those around you with this promise.

My journey through grief showed me the following:

Life is not always fair but it's not personal.

Sometimes it is during the most challenging situations of life that great faith develops.

The Holy Spirit is ALWAYS available to offer assistance. We just need to ask and to listen for that still small voice.

We must think supernaturally:

To trust when things seem so tangled and twisted

To choose joy through difficulties

To follow God wholeheartedly, even when we are unsure of what is ahead.

The necessity to look beyond our ever changing circumstances to the One who is the same, yesterday, today, and forever, to trust God and rest in His sovereignty.

I encourage you to cherish every single moment you have with those you hold dear.

Tell them how much they mean to you and how you love them. Brag on them and emphasize their gifts and talents. Remember always that NO ONE is perfect, including you and to look for and find the positive attributes you see in the ones you love.

You don't want to one day live with regrets because, believe me, you will remember every single thing you wished you had done but didn't.

Don't wait until tomorrow to express your love and gratitude for the people who are close to you.

Don't mistake moving on with life as disloyalty to the ones you have loved. When a loved one dies and we are left behind, our life does NOT end with theirs. God's plan for our life continues.

The grief process is different for every person and manifests itself differently.

There are stages of grief that we go through and it is important to get through those stages in order to begin the healing process.

Laying down and giving up is not what the Lord has in mind for us. In fact, many professionals tell us that if we are unable to move forward within two years after the death of a spouse, we need to evaluate and assess what other factors might be influencing this inability or refusal to move forward.

We must make every effort, and encourage those we minister to, to find a new "normal" and to continue being salt and light to those around us.

ENJOY AND RELISH EVERY SEASON AND EVERY CHAPTER OF YOUR LIFE

Reverend Teena Whaley Culbreth

"A DOZEN ROTTEN EGGS"

By: Reverend Peggy Caldwell

Peggy and her husband Reverend Dean Caldwell, are credentialed ministers in the Assemblies of God, and have served together in ministries and as pastors for many years. They have raised two daughters in the ministry. Peggy has years of experience as a preacher's wife. She is also a retreat speaker, Bible teacher, a prayer warrior, and has an anointed music ministry. She and her husband are well known and loved evangelists ministering across the country.

"This Is My Story"

This experience happened when I was at a time in my life, weary, exhausted and wondering,

"What am I doing? Is this what being a preacher's wife is all about? Believe me, this ain't no picnic and it ain't no life of luxury!"

But then the Lord spoke to me and,

"This is my story".

I opened the refrigerator to check on space to put my coleslaw, when I smelled the awful stench! I thought,

"Oh my goodness, what was the terrible odor?"

There before my eyes was the culprit, "A DOZEN ROTTEN EGGS"! Someone had accidentally hit the control button on the refrigerator and the temperature had been turned to a dangerous amount, way too warm to keep things cold enough to preserve. The eggs had been left over from the Men's Prayer Breakfast and now had ended up ruining on the shelf.

I hurried, took them to the dumpster and began the long ordeal of taking everything out of the refrigerator.

I began washing walls, shelves and compartments with vinegar and water and, anything else I could find to kill that awful odor.

My blood pressure was rising, my mind racing as I talked to myself and complained,

**"Well God, this certainly is not my job! I am,
"THE PASTOR'S WIFE"!**

I have too many other important jobs to be doing especially on Sunday afternoon than to be up here cleaning out this church refrigerator!"

Feeling sorry for myself while telling God my *"sob story"* about how over-worked and unappreciated I was.

I suddenly looked down and saw myself. I was using my hands, moving my shoulder, walking and cleaning, seeing and yes, even smelling. I could do all these things!

"OH GOD, PLEASE FORGIVE ME!"

Had I so quickly forgotten the *"MIRACLE"* that had happened in my life in the past year?

For you see, on February 16, 2000, I was diagnosed with breast cancer. On March 9, 2000, I had a modified radical mastectomy on my left side.

At that moment did not know what my future held!

"Would I be alive Christmas, to spend it with my husband and two daughters?"

"Would I be able to continue to work in the church, ministering to others, as I loved to do?"

"OH, DEAR GOD, I AM SO SORRY,"

I said as I began to weep and cry out to God.

I began to thank God for <u>allowing</u> me the privilege of washing those shelves, walls and compartments of the church's refrigerator.

I could lift and I could clean!

I am alive today!

I am blessed beyond measure, and <u>allowed</u> to clean again for my Lord!

**"PLEASE GOD,
DON'T EVER LET ME FORGET
WHAT YOU HAVE DONE FOR ME!"
Not just on March 9, 2000 but,
Every day that I live,
Because He Lives, I Live Also!**

Reverend Peggy Caldwell

"TEACH YOUR CHILDREN DILIGENTLY"

By: Reverend Trudy Jackson

Trudy was an Assemblies of God Missionary for twenty-three years serving in the South Pacific. She and her husband Reverend Scott Jackson are ordained ministers and have been married for eleven years. Their daughter Shirleyna was six years old when this was written. They pastored International Christian Fellowship and directed Chi Alpha ministry on the College of Micronesia Campus in Pohnpei. They worked with the Federated States of Micronesia, Assemblies of God. Recently they returned to Arkansas to pastor the Assembly of God Church in Lewisville. This story is written for this book.

"FROM THE HEART OF A PASTOR'S WIFE, AND A MOTHER."

Deuteronomy 6:4-9, V4, "Hear, O Israel: The Lord our God is one Lord:"

V5, "Thou shall love the Lord thy God with all thine heart, with all thy soul, and with all thy might."

V6, "And these words, which I command thee this day, shall be in thine heart."

V7, "And thou shall teach them diligently unto thy children, and shalt talk of them when thou sittest in thine house, and when thou walketh by the way, and when thou liest down, and when thou risest up."

V8, "And thou shalt bind them for a sign upon thine hand, and they shall be a frontlets before thine eyes."

V9, "And thou shall write them upon the posts of thy

house, and on thy gates."

At age thirty-eight the Lord brought Scott into my life to become my husband. I was already in the ministry as a single missionary and a pastor. It is such a joy to now serve the Lord together with my husband.

Three years later, the Lord blessed our home with our daughter, Shirleyna. On her delivery day, she came out crying, ready to face the world. That was one of the sweetest sounds. Scott held her first and prayed,

"Lord, make her a prophetess to the nations!"

What an awesome responsibility God has given to us as He has entrusted her into our care. It has been a challenge trying to balance the responsibilities of being a preacher's wife, a mother, a missionary, and a pastor.

As you may know or have experienced as a pastor or pastor's wife, people are always looking to you to be the perfect example. And, I am so far from perfect.

There are times that I can get so overwhelmed with all the responsibilities, especially when Shirleyna was a baby that I just wanted a "Calgon, take me away moment." A dear friend and pastor's wife, Julia Amis, said to me,

"Trudy, people will give you all kinds of advice: some good, some not so good. However, God is the one who made you a mom, and with that, He has given you God-given instincts as a mom. Listen to those God-given instincts in raising Shirleyna."

That was one of the best advice as a mom in ministry that I have ever received. In fact, God's Word tells us in,

Isaiah 54:13, that "And all thy children shall be taught by the Lord; and great shall be the peace of thy children."

Ladies, God wants to teach our children, and He wants to teach them through our lives.

I often pray, and some days many times,

"Lord God, please give me wisdom and knowledge to raise this child."

The Lord is faithful! I just have to put myself in a position where the Lord can speak to me, and teach me, so I can teach my daughter. When Shirleyna was a baby, the Lord dropped this scripture into my heart, to tell her every day. It is from,

Deuteronomy 6:5, paraphrased. "You shall love the Lord God with all your heart, with all your soul, with all your strength, and with all your mind, and you shall love your neighbor as yourself."

Each day, we plead the blood of Jesus over her. At night, we have devotions and prayer with Shirleyna. One prayer my husband Scott began praying was,

"Lord, keep every evil man, woman, boy and girl away from her."

SPIRITUAL COVERING FOR OUR CHILDREN

As Shirleyna got older, if Scott or I didn't pray that, she would remind us and pray that over her own life. Children need and want the Lord's covering over their lives. We have seen how Shirleyna will move away from people or won't warm up to certain people. **And, that is okay, as God can and does give our children discernment too.**

It is not only important for our children to see us pray, but also for them to hear us pray and have them participate in praying with us and for us. One night when she was two, she was praying and she said,

"Babababa Lord Touch Daddy! Babababa, Amen."

She had heard us pray with our understanding and in the Spirit, so, she thought she should too. Don't be afraid to pray in the heavenly language God has given you. One prayer I have prayed even before I got married was,

"Lord, please help me pass along my godly Spirit-filled heritage to my children." Now that I have a child of my own, I still pray that and desire it even more.

One night as I was praying for people to be filled with the Holy Spirit Shirleyna stopped me and said,

"Mommy, pray for me too, that I can have that Holy Spirit thing!"

I say, "YES!!!" We are still praying she will be filled with the Holy Spirit and then *"continually"* be filled with the Holy Spirit.

Children love to be involved with what we are doing, so include them even in the work of the ministry. When Shirleyna was a baby, we would just carry her to the altar with us to pray for people. As she grew older, she would also lay hands on people and pray for them.

One time though, Shirleyna started going for a person's nose, so I had to quickly redirect her little hand. I'm so glad the lady had her eyes closed.

Our children should be a part of our lives and ministry that God has called us to. He wants to use them too.

SPIRITUAL WARFARE:

There is a definite spiritual warfare that rages against God's people, and, it even affects our children. When we sense a spiritual attack in our home, we tell Shirleyna,

"We need to pray our house out!"

We pray with authority and rebuke any evil spirits and command them to leave in Jesus' Name. Then we invite the Holy Spirit to fill our home. We even *"pray out,"* hotels when we stay in them.

I believe children are more in tune to spirits then we are at times. When Shirleyna was five, I was giving her a bath. I left the room for a few minutes then I heard her say,

"I see you."

I was thinking, who or what is she seeing? I listen as she went on to say,

"You get out of here Devil in Jesus Name!"

Later, I asked her about it. She told me that she saw this dark shadow come into the bathroom, and she knew it was of the devil. So she rebuked it in Jesus' name, and then went back to playing.

Children are not too young to teach them how to fight spiritual warfare and take authority in Jesus' name.

It is important to guard what our children watch or listen to. We have tried to fill Shirleyna's heart and mind with many Bible stories by telling her, or using books and DVD's. It was such a blessing when she would play with other children and want them to act out Bible stories with her.

CARTOONS:

Today they are filled with so much witchcraft. There have been times when bad thoughts or images come into Shirleyna's mind. It usually comes from something she has seen or heard, even if it were only for a split second.

We were on a twelve hour flight so, I let her watch "Tom & Jerry", thinking I had watched that as a child and it would be okay.

It wasn't but a few minutes and she tugged at my arm and said,

"Mommy, turn it off, I don't like the witch!"

I thought I was letting her watch something that was safe. The sly devil put something evil in that cartoon. We turned it off. About thirty minutes later, she said,

"Mommy, please pray for me and rebuke those bad thoughts from my mind, because I still see that witch."

So, we took authority over her thoughts in the name of Jesus, and she was fine the rest of the flight.

GIVING:

Another area to teach our children is in the area of, *"giving to others"* and *"giving to God."* We have taught Shirleyna that when she gets money, the first ten percent belongs to the Lord.

One day as we were driving, Shirleyna was three years old at the time. She was sitting in the back of our vehicle with two quarters in her hand. All of a sudden she said.

"Caesar's, Caesar's, God's, God's."

The Lord was reminding her that He deserves His part of our money.

OBEDIENCE:

Obedience is a big spiritual truth that we must teach our children, because if we love God, than we will obey Him. God's Word says in,

Ephesians 6:1, "Children obey your parents in the Lord for this is right."

We are still in the process of teaching her that when she disobeys she is really disobeying God because He tells children to obey their parents.

I have also tried to make a connection with her that she not only needs to ask us to forgive her, but she needs to ask God for forgiveness each time she sins. And yes, God forgives us, but there can still be consequences for our sins.

There are more spiritual things we need to teach our children; however, if we will listen, often, the Lord teaches us those lessons through our children.

In closing this story, we had just boarded a plane to go back overseas. Shirleyna was quite wiggly, and I told her to set back in her seat. She looked at me sweetly and said,

"And enjoy the flight."

May the Lord help us all to enjoy the journey of:
Being a mother, and Being a mother in ministry, and
Being a preacher's wife

Reverend Trudy Jackson

"WORDS OF WISDOM FROM A MISSIONARY'S CHILD"

By: Miss Shirleyna Jackson.

Shirleyna is the daughter of, Reverends Scott and Trudy Jackson. They were Assemblies of God Missionaries in Pohnpei, Micronesia. She is wise beyond her years in the ways of the Lord. Shirleyna is a missionary at heart. More and more we see that God is speaking through little children and that they have a personal relationship with Him. Scripture records that a little child shall lead them. She was five years old, and in the first grade when this incident occurred. Recently, her parents returned to Arkansas and became pastors of the Lewisville Assembly of God Church.

Isaiah 11:6, "......... and a little child shall lead them."

"Shirleyna's Desire: What I Want To Be!"

Shirleyna asked her dad if he thought she was fat. Scott said,

"No! Why?"

She responded by telling us of a conversation she had with one of the neighbor girls.

The girl asked her if she wanted to be fat or skinny. Shirleyna told us that she told the girl,

**"I don't want to be fat and
I don't want to be skinny.
I just want to be the way God prepared me to be!"**

Miss Shirleyna Jackson

Proverbs 22:6, "Train up a child in the way he should go: and when he is old, he will not depart from it."

"AN EPISODE IN THE LIFE OF A PASTOR'S WIFE"

By: Reverend Wanda Huie

Wanda and her husband Reverend Bob Huie are well known and loved across Arkansas. Both are Ordained Assemblies of God Ministers. They pastored churches and evangelized together for many years until Brother Huie was called home to be with Jesus. Wanda has served as The Assistant Arkansas District Women's Ministries Director for nine years, and as The Women's Ministries Director for eight years. She continues to minister to, and encourage women as the Lord directs her life.

"LEARNING: TO LOVE AGAIN"

Harmony is a beautiful thing. I prayed everywhere we served as pastors that harmony would prevail in all functions of the church and at all times. But that is a very rare thing indeed. One is rarely, if ever prepared for discord, especially when it comes unexpectedly.

We were serving as pastors in a North Texas City. The church was in the process of building a parsonage. Every free moment Bob and our young son Eddie were working on it. On this specific occasion the hole for the septic tank was being dug. The ground was very rocky and huge rocks were in the ground. It took manual labor to chip away the rock and remove it from the hole and then haul it away.

Bob worked endlessly alone day after day chipping away at the rocky hole until one day the hole was finally deep enough to set the septic tank in the ground and cover it before the weather became worse.

The superintendent of the project was a church member, but was unable to help with the building process. He was responsible for ordering all supplies for the finishing of the parsonage.

About the time Bob had the septic tank hole dug, the superintendent of the job became ill and had to go to the hospital. To keep from delaying the project at the parsonage, Bob assumed the responsibility of ordering the septic tank himself. Apparently, it was the wrong thing to do. When Bob told the Superintendent of the job about ordering the septic tank, the man became irate and replied,

"What if I had already ordered the septic tank?"

There was no reasoning with this brother.

This was a family church with over half of the congregation being related. The relatives and those close to the relatives instantly became very disenchanted with the parsonage family. An apology did not help.

In small churches often the congregation will volunteer to do a general cleaning of the church to keep operating expenses down. It was the fall of the year, and on this particular night, a good group showed up to clean. Everyone was extremely quiet.

I spoke to several but there was no response. This continued for a time. Then one of the ladies, who was not a relative, and did not share the others thoughts and feelings regarding the septic tank episode pulled me aside and asked, if I would like to know what was going on? Of course I would!

She told me that it was all because Bob had neglected to go through the parsonage building superintendent before ordering the septic tank. A BITTER LESSON LEARNED!

At the church on the following Sunday morning, the atmosphere was strained. People huddled in small groups whispering. The Sunday school office was so crowded it was impossible to get in or out. We all got the message of course. By then the majority of the church was not speaking to any of our family.

We decided then that we could no longer be of further use to the church. Bob drove to a nearby city, found a job and we moved a few weeks before Christmas.

A few of the members of the church knew nothing about all that was going on until the following Sunday when Bob resigned. There were expressions of shock on faces of those who had heard nothing of what was happening. They felt detached from being a part of the church.

I learned that something done in innocence can develop into the loss of something precious and good. We lost the fellowship and friendship of some wonderful people. It also created pain and disappointment for a congregation. The church suffered badly as well as our family.

I hurt for them and I hurt for us. Our children were so bewildered they could scarcely comprehend what was happening and Bob was hurting deeply I know.

Being ostracized is one of my most painful experiences. Looking back over that experience after many years, my initial response was to guard my heart and not let anyone get close enough to hurt me like that again.

Years later, and we were pastoring another church. I was meeting with the Women's Ministries group one Sunday night. It was a type of open ended questions. I had come to care deeply for these people, but still held myself aloof for my own protection.

Someone mentioned they thought that I really didn't care about them. I was very honest with them explaining the story above to them and how hurt I had been and that I couldn't bear that to happen again.

They prayed for me, and after that prayer, the Lord opened up my heart to them all the way. We had a wonderful ministry in that place.

I have learned to love again without reservations. Through this experience, I learned you can't judge the people in one church by the people in another church the same.

I have learned that problems don't come in the same way and that, not everyone is insecure or insensitive.

I have learned to be more sensitive to others feelings, and anticipate their thoughts and their reactions before hearing what I have to say.

I must admit, there are times when I fail to do so, and I genuinely regret it.

I have learned too, that you don't learn it all in one experience.

It takes a lifetime of them,
Because, I am still learning

Reverend Wanda Huie

"FEELING INADEQUATE"

By: Reverend Pam Johnson

Pam and her husband Reverend Bobby L. Johnson ministered together for over fifty years. They served in District leadership positions and pastored Van Buren First Assembly of God Church for thirty-five years, until he was called to his heavenly home. As Pastor's Wife she did what she could: she supported her husband, raised two children, both are in ministries, provided loving care to the congregation, and ministers to women incarcerated, Most of all, she follows God's plan for her life day by day.

"Seeking The Wisdom Of Other Preacher's Wives"

When Bobby started in the ministry fifty plus years ago, I recognized quickly how little I knew and, that I needed help and needed it now! I felt so inadequate since I didn't play the piano or wasn't an accomplished teacher, nor could I hit a home run at church camp. So I did what I knew to do, and that was to just be myself!

I talked to Sister Gotcher and my mother in law Sister Leila Johnson. Both were pastor's wives. If there was something I was unsure of I would call them. They gave me godly wisdom and kept me from making a fool of myself many times. All of us need someone to bounce things off of. Especially if they had crossed those hurdles, they could surely help me!

Each stressed: get up in the morning and make yourself and your house presentable. And now even after all these years, I make my bed as I get out of it. I am still working on making myself presentable and together at the crack of dawn.

I still work on measuring my words and guarding what I say.

One night Bobby woke me up and told me that I was grinding my teeth.

I told him it was for all the things that I couldn't say during the day. I knew if I kept quiet I wouldn't have to apologize. But, I still had to pray through to keep my heart and mind clean.

People always expect your kids to be perfect. We are a close family and I warned them of their actions, but NEVER expected them to be the example, but to love and serve the Lord because of their own personal commitment to Him.

That would be the blessing to their dad and to the church.

One day when they were teenagers, a man in the church called for my husband to come and pray for him. But, Bobby was not at home. Later, when he came home, Torin said,

"Dad, Brother Satterfield called and you weren't here so I went over and prayed for him."

Dara did the same. They loved sharing in the ministry.

We tried to have treat night ever so often and would have them choose where to go, and what to eat.

(Phones were turned off, and they had our undivided attention.)

We did not want them to resent the ministry, and made sure they had their own time with us.

Make your home a haven: A place where your husband and kids can relax and unwind. Have family prayer time. These have been some of the sweetest times for all of us.

LIVE YOUR LIFE, AND ENJOY THE MINISTRY.
KEEP IT POSITIVE!
YOUR CHILDREN WILL TAKE THEIR CUE FROM YOU.

Pray constantly for your husband that God will bless, protect, and give him wisdom.

Get solidly behind him as he preaches, and prays.

Most of all, Keep those white shirts ironed.

(Bobby always wore white shirts)!!!

And on that day may the Lord say,

"Well Done thou good and faithful:
mother, pastor's wife, cook, carpooler,
cleaner and gardener."
Enjoy your ministry and your life.

Reverend Pam Johnson

"LIFE IS: ONLY AS GOOD AS YOUR MINDSET."

By: Reverend Jane Powell Carpenter

Jane and her husband Reverend Harold Powell ministered together for many years until he was called to his heavenly home. She prayerfully saught God for her future. In God's providence she married Reverend Tommy Carpenter, former Arkansas District Secretary-Treasurer and Missions Director. Both are credentialed ministers with The Assemblies of God. They have served as missionaries to Belize where they organized teams for construction of facilities, and began "Jane's Feeding Program" in Frank's Eddy Village. Jane is well known as a Bible teacher, preacher, musician, and retreat speaker. Together they have served as interem pastors of several churches and continue fulfilling God's call on their lives.

"Becoming Bitter or Better"

The book of Ruth in the Bible records how Naomi's mindset changed while she was in Moab, for there she was widowed. Also, while in Moab her two sons died and she was left alone with their wives.

As you read this account in the book of Ruth, it is evident that difficult circumstances played a role in Naomi's actions. She changed her name from **"NAOMI, TO BITTER".**

She declared her identity according to her circumstances. She changed her perception of God. Naomi said:

"God is against me. I left full and came back empty!"

When my pastor husband became ill and eventually grew worse, I had to assume the role of pastor and work full time in order to provide health insurance. This role included cleaning the church, playing the keyboard, teaching class, preparation and delivery of sermons and the list goes on.

After his passing, I continued to pastor our church for over a year before moving to Florida. There, I discovered my outdoor prayer closet. In our gated community I walked, rode my bike, or drove to a nearby undeveloped paved area.

Each evening for two years, this quarter of a mile circular drive was my "special" place of prayer. The sunsets in the west were often filled with an unbelievable fiery blaze of clouds. At times, I felt as though I could literally walk into heaven itself if a ladder had been available.

Upon returning to Arkansas, Mt. Nebo became my next prayer closet. Afternoons and late evenings were spent on the mountain reading the Word, walking, and praying about my future. The Word provided insight and content for my prayers.

Most nights I witnessed the lights appear in the valley, the deer casually strolling about the picnic area and then, I knew it was time to go home, maneuvering the sharp curves of the downward spiral in the dark.

During my prayer time in that "special prayer closet", I asked the Lord over and over,

"What do you want to do with me? Where do I go?"

Time passed. I ascended my mountain, my new prayer closet for another two years. God was working in my behalf even though I didn't realize it.

I remember asking the Lord *often* to do something with me that was *mightier* than I could do for myself. I prayed for four things:

For Purpose, For Place, For People, and For Provision.

God answered in an unexpected way. November 8, 2013 I married a great man of God. Reverend Tommy Carpenter and we vowed to commit the rest of our lives serving the Lord together. Three days later, I arrived in Belize!

This was indeed *mightier* than I could do for myself! I could not, in my human flesh, have charted my course in this direction.

Two years in Florida at my outdoor prayer closet, then two more years on Mt. Nebo, praying and waiting, God worked in my life.

Naomi was so changed by her circumstances, that when she arrived home, her friends did not recognize her.

No doubt her countenance, posture, and speech were different. This was not the Naomi they knew. She changed from: *"pleasant to bitter,"* and *"full to empty"* because she allowed the difficult circumstances to twist her perception of God.

Naomi's inaccurate perception of God affected four areas:

1. It produced a destructive change in the way she viewed her identity.

2. Her words and outlook became negative.

3. Her natural mindset clouded her counsel to others.

4. Her advice could have derailed Ruth's future and God's plan.

Naomi believed Ruth's future depended on *her ability* rather than God's leading. With her natural mindset, she instructed the girls:

"You will be better off to return to Moab. I'm too old to have more sons. You wouldn't wait for them to grow up." *She declared,* "I'm no use to you."

God's plan was: for Ruth to be in the lineage of Jesus. Naomi's Mindset was: in opposition to the mind of God and a threat to the plan and provision of God.

Pastor's Wives, have *"response choices"* to make when unpleasant or inconvenient circumstances appear.

I chose to find my prayer closet at my place of abode, wherever that might be. When your ability to: *"Fix, and Make Happen"* or *"Cause to Be"* is limited. You must not see your life as hopeless, for then, you will tackle life in the natural with human limitations.

There are no hopeless situations: only people who have grown hopeless about that situation. When your *natural* is hopeless, remember what God can do in the *spiritual realm.* God *can* and *will* do in the *spiritual* that which you cannot do in the *natural realm.*

God has a plan for you, and that plan is much larger than your circumstances. Going from *full to empty,* can change the course of history for you and for those around you. Naomi's perception could have changed the course of history for Ruth.

"Pastor's Wives" are placed in the unique position to affect many lives. Sometimes they can be used in another country in ways never dreamed possible!

"Jane's Feeding Program" in *Frank's Eddy Village, Belize,* is just one example, And, YES, God answered my prayers.

He gave me: PURPOSE, PLACE, AND PROVISION. All at once, because: He sent a very special person to me.

Here's a portion of a poem, I composed long ago.

A few lines read like this:

"IN HIS IMAGE"

Arise, daughter
Let me share
That when you've hurt
I've been there.
Touched your cheek,
Stroked your hair,

You're a Woman of Worth,
I attended your birth.
Your force and your power
Know no limitations
When you...only you,
Set your mind to it!

Reverend Jane Powell

"LED STEP BY STEP, KEEPING MY VOWS TO GOD"

By: Reverend Nadine Waldrop

Nadine began ministering in her local church working with girls ages twelve to seventeen. God gave her a vision for ministry to Native Americans and led her step by step into that ministry. She faced dangerous situations on reservations as a single woman pastor. She vowed to God that she would not marry unless to a single man called to the same ministry as she was. She remained a single woman keeping her vows to God. As an Ordained Assemblies of God Missionary, Nadine touched thousands of young lives during the thirty-six years of ministry at the American Indian Bible College, (now S.A.G.U. American Indian College).

"KEEPING MY VOWS MADE TO GOD AS A SINGLE WOMAN IN THE MINISTRY"

In 1957, our family moved to Glendale, Arizona and began attending First Assembly of God Church. Shortly after that, I helped to start a girl's club known as Missionettes for girls ages twelve to seventeen. The next year, we got permission from our pastor to have a revival for the girls.

A young girl in the church, Alice Young, was an evangelist with her brother. Pastor Smith said we could have services but not to interfere with the regular church services. So, we had service on Tuesday, Thursday and Friday. God was blessing mightily so we got permission to go another week.

On Thursday of the second week, while I was praying, God gave me a vision of my working with dark-skinned people who lived in what I realized later were wickiups *(a tee-pee shaped dwelling used by the White Mountain Apache Tribe).*

In April of 1959, I went with a family in our church to Canyon Day for the weekend.

Sister Gilman, the missionary's wife, told me of a need for someone to visit patients in the Phoenix Indian Hospital. At that time, there was no hospital on the reservation, only a clinic. People were often transported to Phoenix, and there was nobody they knew to visit and pray with them.

I immediately told her that I would do it. That is where my ministry to Native Americans began. I continued with hospital ministry at the Phoenix Indian Medical Center for approximately seven years.

Later in 1966 Reverend and Mrs. Leo Gilman asked me to work with them at Canyon Day Assembly of God Church. Canyon Day is about five miles from Whiteriver, The Tribal Center of The White Mountain Apaches in Eastern Arizona.

I really wanted to be in God's will, but didn't know how to tell my parents that I wanted to quit my job and go into full time ministry.

I became ill and was admitted to the hospital. For three days, my head kept turning from side to side. The doctors could not find what was wrong. On the third day, I told God I would do His will and go into full time ministry. That same day, my head stopped turning and I was released from the hospital.

The following has been on my mind for several days, so I thought I would send it to you. I don't know if it is important or not, but it was to me.

I often talk to young people about making a vow to God.

> *Deuteronomy 23:21-23, "When thou shalt vow a vow unto the Lord thy God, thou shalt not slack to pay it: for*

the Lord thy God will surely require it of thee; and it would be sin in thee."

V22, "But if thou shalt forbear to vow, it shall be no sin in thee."

V23, "That which is gone out of thy lips thou shalt keep and perform; even a freewill offering, according as thou hast vowed unto the Lord thy God, which thou hast promised with thy mouth."

I have thought of that verse many times. When God first called me into Native American Ministries, I vowed that I would not marry unless I found a single man that was called to the same ministry as I was.

I never found that man. I have kept my vow to God through all these years. God has blessed me abundantly for keeping my word and promise to Him.

NOTE: *God keeps His promises to us, how much more should we keep our vows and promises to Him? One must be cautious in making vows to God. Many have made foolish vows and just forgot them. God requires that we pay or keep those vows we make to Him.*

While I was working at Canyon Day, I felt the need to apply for ministerial credentials. I met with the Arizona District Officials of the Assemblies of God to begin that process.

I remember Brother Gressett, the Arizona District Superintendent told me not to go up there and fall in love with one of those "young bucks".

I assured him that I made a vow to God that I would not marry unless I found a single man who shared the same calling as me. As of the age of seventy-eight years, I have not met that man. Therefore I have remained single. This has proved to be a blessing many times.

Due to some health issues, I had to return home early in 1968, from working at Canyon Day. My doctor told me I could not go back to the reservation but could go back to work, so, I returned to work in the bank.

In 1970, I began assisting Paul and Kathy Cagle, Missionaries on the Gila River Indian Community.

We actually had services in the nearby community of Laveen, Arizona. We moved to a family's home on the reservation where we had services for about three years.

Each Sunday, we moved the family furniture to the sides and set up *"church furniture".* After service, we would move it all back again.

Later, the Cagles accepted the pastorate at Salt River, *(another Indian community east of Phoenix)* and moved to that reservation.

The Arizona District Officials asked if I wanted to be the senior pastor, and I accepted. I pastored there until June 1979. During that time, I faced much criticism for being a woman preacher, but I knew I was in God's will. The church grew both numerically and spiritually.

Also, during that time, I faced numerous times of danger. My house was burglarized three times. Several other times a man broke into my house and waited outside for me to return. Fortunately, his sister and niece were with me each time and stayed with me until after he left the area. On other occasions, they spent the night with me.

After all this, the District Officials told me I should leave for my own safety. Of course, God had everything under control. At the time I was leaving the reservation, a bookkeeping position opened at American Indian Bible College, now (S.A.G.U. American Indian College).

I had a bookkeeping background so I applied for the position. I was hired immediately and began working the next week. During the thirty-six years I was at the College, I served in various positions.

Since I was single, I was asked to accompany students on missions trips and to host other single ladies who came to minister.

I am still a U. S. Missionary to Native Americans and love to serve wherever I can. I still assist at the College. I enjoy visiting and ministering with our alumni in the local area and on various reservations.

During these years, God has been with me and allowed me to minister in so many different ways.

I do not regret being a single woman in ministry.

I have not had much negative talk to me about being a single woman preacher. The one time I can think of was the pastor of my home church. He felt it was okay for a woman to be a missionary, but not to be a pastor. Not sure about his thinking.

God led me step by step to the places He chose for me to minister. He gave me rapport with those I ministered to.

I am so glad I said "Yes" to the Lord
When God asked me to be
His minister

Reverend Nadine Waldrop

"IT'S A GREAT LIFE, BEING A "PASTOR'S WIFE"

By: Mrs. Barbara Blann

Barbara has ministered side by side with her preacher husband Reverend Laron Blann for over fifty-six years. They have pastored three Assemblies of God Churches, the last one for forty-two years, until their retirement due to physical issues. She was the church pianist, and continues as a Bible Teacher. She also followed a nursing career where she ministered to both physical and spiritual needs of her patients.

"MY GRACE IS SUFFICIENT TO GET YOU THROUGH!"

As I sit here thinking, pondering and meditating on what to share I don't know where to start but at the beginning of my Christian walk. I was saved at the very young age of fourteen. When I was sixteen years old, I married the already "called" minister, Reverend Laron Blann.

We had been married only four months when we were offered the pastorate of a small country church. We accepted that ministry position.

We *"grew"* during that time and we pastored there eight and one half years. I knew nothing about the role of a "Pastor's Wife". It was a step by step, and a day by day learning experience.

While there, I taught the beginner class and learned to play the piano. Three of our beautiful children were born during our time at this church. I walked with Jesus and He taught me as I grew up and grew in the Lord.

Our next ministry position was for five years. Here, I assumed the role of pianist and taught the Teen Class. I said,

"LORD HELP ME!"

I learned even more while teaching them. I listened with my ears and my heart. Without even realizing it, I became a role model to some of the teens.

With each day that passed, I learned more and more to just live for Jesus and love Him. He taught me that He would never fail me. During the good times, the joyful times, and at the very low times of my life Jesus was my rock, my refuge, my strength, and He was my everything.

In 1974 God spoke to our hearts to move again. This was our third and final church. There is no doubt God called us. We remained at First Assembly of God Church at Fordyce, Arkansas as senior pastors for forty-two years. Not too long after our move, our last baby was born. All our children graduated from the schools there.

During this time of ministry, we dedicated babies, married them, and dedicated their babies. Recently we retired due to my husband's health issues. It is an awesome church that we loved with all our hearts. We have laughed with our church family, and we have cried with them also.

Has it always been easy? "NO!" Life is never easy. But, when Jesus Christ is in our boat, He calms the storms that arise in our lives. I have learned that even the storms obey His command.

In September of 1994, we started building a new church building. The same month, I was diagnosed with breast cancer. I went through surgery and Chemotherapy. I guess it was one of the lowest times of my life. Since surgery and Chemo threw me into a weakened and discouraged state. I remember asking God,

"WHY ME? I HAVE LIVED FOR YOU ALL MY LIFE!"

God gently spoke to me,

"WHY NOT YOU,
MY GRACE IS SUFFICIENT TO GET YOU THROUGH!"

Our precious church family surrounded me and helped me up when I was weak and broken hearted. God's Word tells us that He is close to the broken hearted.

> *Psalms 34:18-19, "The Lord is neigh unto them that are of a broken heart; and saveth such as be of a contrite spirit."*

> *V19, "Many are the afflictions of the righteous: but the Lord delivereth him out of them all."*

I entered a period of depression and self-pity for about two weeks and soon realized that I did not like that place because:

No one comes to a pity party but you and Satan!

I shook myself and decided that me and Jesus could do this. That was twenty-three years ago, and I am still working for Him.

Along with being wife, mom and being pastor's wife, I went to nursing school and have had a nursing career for thirty-six years. The joy of my life, was being a nurse, and being a pastor's wife.

As a nurse, I tend to the physical needs of people. As a pastor's wife, I could tend to the spiritual needs of people. Sometimes, I have the privilege to minister to both needs at the same time. I can usually manage to speak a word for Jesus to patients and encourage the ones who were bruised and beaten down by life and its obstacles.

One thing I have learned as a "Pastor's Wife" of fifty-six years is I could have friends in the church. But most of all, I learned the necessity of being "VERY" careful with my words and comments.

I've been blessed to have never had any conflict with church members. I contribute that blessing to my favorite slogan,

"YOU CAN'T MISQUOTE SILENCE!"

Be ever so mindful of your words. They can't be taken back!

> *Proverbs 18:21, "Death and life are in the power of the tongue: and they that love it shall eat the fruit thereof. "*

My advice to every "Pastor's wife" is to:

Love Jesus with all your heart, soul, mind and strength and God will hold you close and speak to your heart. We just need to learn to listen. He will *"never"* lead us astray.

Jesus has the answer before you knew you had a problem. Recognize the still small voice and the nudging of the Spirit of God. Become sensitive to His Spirit.

There have been some rough times, but after fifty-six years I have seen that God will *"always"* take care of us. The joys so out-weigh the troubles.

As we were getting close to retirement, our church blessed us with the deed to the parsonage. What a joy, what a blessing to not have to look for a home and move.

I have loved being a "Pastor's Wife" and raising our four beautiful children in what some people call *"a fish bowl", the parsonage.*

I wouldn't trade this life I've had for all the silver and gold this world has to offer.

**I pray that these words
will encourage everyone who reads them**

Mrs. Barbara Blann

"BACK TO THE BASICS"

By: Reverend Angelia Carpenter

Angelia is well known and loved in the Arkansas District Assemblies of God. She has served as the District Women's Ministries Director for ten years. She and her Husband Reverend Thomas Carpenter are ordained ministers. They have served as pastors, conducted Children's Crusades, and various other ministries including Sponsors of "Buck's Toys Ministry", providing toys for Africa's Children. They presently serve as Assemblies of God Missionaries to "Special Needs Ministries."

"MY CIRCUMSTANCES DON'T CHANGE WHO GOD IS!"

In my young life of nearly fifty years, I have found myself going back to the basics during those times of doubt and worry. **In other words, going back to what I know to be true, timeless, tested and unchanging.**

Of those few basic foundations of life, I will share three. I did not read these in a book, although I'm sure someone has probably penned them before me. I did not hear them in a sermon again someone has undoubtedly preached the same in some fashion or another. No, God gave me these phrases one day in prayer when I surely needed them the most! Doesn't He have perfect timing?

Our eight year old son, along with my sweet mother-in-law, my good friend of twenty-five years, had both been killed in a car accident not three months prior. I can't recall many details of that prayer time, except to say that I was listening.

There's a time to cry out, and believe me, I had done that countless times. Then, there is a time to listen. I must add the fact that brokenness puts you in a position to listen at least it did for me.

Right alongside that fact, is that I was so broken that on many occasions I didn't know what to say in prayer.

Sometimes, you just breathe or grown in prayer, that's okay. The Holy Spirit understands completely. One fact we can all agree on is that you have to be quiet to listen.

> *Psalms 46:10, <u>"Be still, and know that I am God</u>: I will be exalted among the heathen, I will be exalted in the earth."*

SSSHHH! ..... BREATHE! ..... BE STILL! ..... LISTEN!

"MY CIRCUMSTANCES DON'T CHANGE WHO GOD IS!"

God is still God. He is not suddenly "not God" because our son for whom we prayed five years is gone from this earth, or because something unexpected or unwanted happened. God is the one thing that doesn't change in my life, God is God: period! My circumstances, past, present or future can never change that! He always has been and He always will be! That's a comfort and a stronghold to build my life on!

Before going on to #2, you will notice that all three of these start with: **"MY CIRCUMSTANCES DON'T CHANGE"**, I believe the Lord spoke that way to me intentionally because many times we trust God until *"THAT"* happens.

Whatever your "THAT" is: it could be someone passing away, or a relationship ending, that you thought would last forever. Maybe you've experienced a job change, a financial crisis or physical illness.

We're okay trusting God until *"the big one"* hits and then that changes everything! Suddenly, we doubt that God even cares, knows or even exists. Well believe it or not, God is still God!

His Omniscience is not subject to, or affected by our circumstances. They, however devastating, can never change who He is. I for one am so thankful for that.

"MY CIRCUMSTANCES DON'T CHANGE GOD'S POWER!"

We say,

"Lord, don't you see what I'm going through? Have you suddenly become, weak, unfeeling, uncaring and unable to hear my prayer?"

He is **Omnipotent:** that means all powerful. What happens to me cannot weaken His strength or ability to move on my behalf. Really! What it comes down to many times is that we like to feel in control. Then something happens that we couldn't control, so we look to blame someone, in this case GOD, for apparently not being in control, for we think,

"IF YOU WERE IN CONTROL, THEN THIS WOULDN'T HAVE HAPPENED! WOULD IT?"

Missionary and author, Elisabeth Elliot said,

"It is faith and faith alone that can believe things fit into a pattern for good,"

Well spoken by a great woman of faith whose husband was killed by the very people he endeavored to share the Gospel with. Her circumstances did not change *"GOD'S POWER"*, nor did it change my final point.

"MY CIRCUMSTANCES DON'T CHANGE THE FINAL OUTCOME!"

Absolutely nothing can change what God has already written in His Holy Word.

We know how this ends for the believer in Christ. Jesus is the forever ultimate victor! For those of us who are on His team, there are two little words that perfectly describe our future. My husband suggested these two words when I was contemplating what should be written on canvas that had a heaven scene on it, **"WE WIN!"**

I had to agree! Our family members went to heaven in a way that seemed tragic, but the truth is, the bottom line is no matter what,

"WE STILL WIN!"

This describes our future in Christ. We know the final outcome after this life. Because of what Jesus did for us, we will be together forever with those who have gone before us.

THIS IS: "OUR BLESSED HOPE!"

According to **Romans Chapter 5, it is a hope that cannot disappoint us!** (Please read chapter 5)

I hope these three little phrases have encouraged you. They have encouraged and challenged me repeatedly!

LET'S GO "BACK TO THE BASICS",
And build our lives on what we know to be true:
MY CIRCUMSTANCES DON'T CHANGE:
"WHO GOD IS"
"GOD'S POWER"
OR
"THE FINAL OUTCOME",
"WE WIN!"

Reverend Angelia Carpenter

THANKS TO EACH OF YOU

"WOMEN OF GOD"

FOR SHARING WORDS OF WISDOM FROM YOUR HEART:

Thank you so much for making time in your busy schedules to share your heart with other preachers, preacher's wives, women and men in ministry, including those who serve in any area of Christian leadership.

The Holy Spirit has anointed you with a word from God for those Called or Chosen by God to be His ministers.

There is so much hurt, and conflict in our world and even in some churches.

There is also much hurt and discouragement in the lives of many ministers, minister's wives and their families. Some have even considered leaving the ministry.

What you have shared will touch hearts and lives of all who read your message.

Your words of encouragement will inspire and make a difference in so many lives.

Thank you for being willing to open your hearts to others in the Ministry.

You are making a difference for the cause of Christ.

Thank you and God bless you and your ministry.

Reverend Alice Palmer Hill

Chapter 10

PURPOSE OF THE CALL

A MESSAGE FROM GOD

Abram received a message from the Lord calling upon him to separate himself from his old associations and go forth into a new country. The message from God changed his life forever.

> **Genesis 12: 1, "Now the Lord had said unto Abram, "Get thee out of thy country, and from thy kindred, and from thy father's house, unto a land that I will show thee:"**

I can almost hear his wife Sarai, when he told her that God had called him to leave his family and go to some new country.

Put yourself in her place for a few moments. Can you imagine the conversation? What would it be like at your house? Sarai probably said,

SARAI: "Abram are you really sure that it was God speaking to you? You say God spoke to you and told you to pack up and leave our family and all our friends? Tell me, where did God tell you that we should go?"

ABRAM: "I do not know Sarai! God just said we were to go unto a *land that He would show us."*

SARAI: "GO WHERE? How will we know when we get there if we don't know where we are going?"

ABRAM: "God just said we should go! I know the future is unsure, however, God promised He would show me the place when we got there. We must trust Him and His wisdom, so let us be obedient and follow where He leads us."

It took **COMMITMENT** and trust for both of them to obey, pack up, leave family and friends, and follow God from place to place wherever He led them.

Does this sound somewhat familiar? When God called you and your husband, or a single woman into the ministry the future may have seemed uncertain.

Yet, you made the **COMMITMENT** to follow where He leads: to places He chooses for you to minister; where He promises to provide for; and to anoint with the Holy Spirit, as you fulfill His call to the ministry.

COMMITMENT DEFINED: Dedication, faithfulness, an agreement, a decision or willingness to give your time and energy to a cause. The chief commitment of our lives is to God Himself. Matthew 22:37-38.

> *Matthew 22:37-38 V37, "Jesus said unto him, "Thou shalt love the Lord thy God with all thy heart, and with all thy soul, and with all thy mind."*
>
> *V38, "This is the first and great commandment."*
>
> *Acts26:16, "But rise and stand upon thy feet: <u>for I have appeared unto thee for this purpose, to make thee a</u>*

minister and a witness both of these things which thou hast seen, and those things in the which I will appear unto thee,"

1 Peter 5:2, "Feed the flock of God which is among you, taking the oversight thereof, not by constraint, but willingly; not for filthy lucre, but of a ready mind;"

Acts 20:28, "Take heed therefore unto yourselves, and to all the flock, over the which the Holy Ghost hath made you overseers, to feed the Church of God, which He hath purchased with His own blood ."

Signs of the times are everywhere. Prophesies are being fulfilled right before our eyes. This tells us that our time is short to reach the lost, and for the preparation of the saints for His coming. This is no time for today's church to become lukewarm and comfortable just ministering to each other.

In the early church, When God saw that their vision for souls had become blurred; He allowed them to go through persecution. He scattered them everywhere so the Gospel would be preached to all nations and to all people. **THIS IS THE MISSION OF HIS CHURCH AND, THE PURPOSE OF HIS CALL.**

THE MINISTRY IS NOT FOR WHIMPS!

Matthew 10:16, "Beloved, I send you forth as sheep in the midst of wolves: be ye therefore wise as serpents and harmless as doves."

2 Timothy 1:7, "For God has not given us the spirit of fear; but of power, and of love, and of a sound mind."

Know and recognize your enemy. It is not your congregation, your neighbor, or your family member. **IT IS SATAN!**

Use your God given wisdom and faith to recognize the devil's mission: his weapons, and his traps, to come against *all* his fiery darts.

> *Ephesians 6:16, "Above all, taking the shield of faith, wherewith ye SHALL be able to quench ALL, the fiery darts of the wicked."*

> *Romans 12:3 "For I say, "Through the grace given unto me, to every man that is among you, not to think of himself more highly than he ought to think; but to think soberly, according as <u>God has dealt to every man the measure of faith."</u>*

<u>God has dealt to every man the measure of faith.</u> The more you use your faith, the stronger it will become in your life.

> *Matthew 10:1, "And when He had called unto Him His twelve disciples,<u> He gave them power against unclean spirits, to cast them out, and to heal all manner of sickness and all manner of disease."</u>*

PULLING DOWN SATAN'S STRONGHOLDS

A STRONGHOLD IS: *a demonic fortress of thoughts, housing evil spirits that control and influence your attitudes and behavior to distress and discourage you. To influence your view or reaction to situations, circumstances or people, that are contrary to God's will.*

Pastors, Pastor's Wife, Women in Ministry and Leadership you are Satan's prime targets. If negative thoughts or behaviors become repetitive, that is a signal that Satan is building himself a stronghold in your life.

The Bible gives instructions for pulling down his strongholds. Identify the situation in your life that Satan is using and bring it into obedience to Christ.

> **2 Corinthians 10:4-5, *"For the weapons of our warfare are not carnal, but mighty through God to the pulling down of strongholds."***
>
> **V5, *"Casting down imaginations, and every high thing that exalteth itself against the knowledge of God, and <u>bringing into captivity every thought to the obedience of Christ;"</u>***

SPIRITUAL WARFARE AND THE CHILD OF GOD

Satan has declared a spiritual warfare on the church, and is unleashing his wrath on ministers, and the Children of God.

NOTE: Have you ever experienced a time when you were confronted with so many situations designed to destroy your faith and confidence in God, to discourage you and take your mind off spiritual things, and on to the stuff going on around you?

The closer you draw to God, the more Satan fights against you by bringing trouble and hardships to take your heart and mind off of your call, and your relationship with God.

For example: Satan attacks physically, financially, and spiritually, causing all matter of disruptive problems to confront you:

Like, when loved ones suffered with cancer; when raccoons tore up my roof and got into my attic; when rats chewed into our house and destroyed the water line and flooded the carpet. My computer crashed, and I had to replace some of the manuscript of this book.

One thing after the other, oh yes, the devil is the master distractor and the master of discouragement.

Thank the Lord, we are rid of all the critters, repairs are made, and once again our home is a place of peace and joy filled with the presence of God.

When we recognize the devil's tactics, we take our God given authority over him and the situation declaring:

"That's enough Satan! No more! Stop your attack on me, my family, and my household. I resist you and you have to flee, in Jesus Name, the Name above all names."

NOTE: Please read these scriptures over and over until they get into your spirit. They are given to help us to be victorious day by day.

> *1 Peter 5:8-11, V8, "Be sober, be vigilant; because your adversary the devil, as a roaring lion, walketh about, seeking whom he may devour."*
>
> *V9, "Whom resist steadfast in the faith, knowing that the same afflictions are accomplished in your brethren that are in the world."*
>
> *V10, "But the God of All grace, who hath called us unto His Eternal Glory by Christ Jesus, after that ye have suffered a while, make you perfect, stablish, strengthen, settle you."*
>
> *V11, "To Him be glory and dominion forever and ever. Amen."*

Sometimes when we are weak, we begin to drift along with the tide. I thank God that He sent a wakeup call, a message to me that turned

His search light on my soul.

He opened my spiritual eyes, and showed me that I was indeed drifting from my first love, and if I would return, He would restore what was lost.

I wept in repentance before Him, and allowed Him to heal the brokenness that had overtaken me.

I am so thankful that the Holy Spirit continually watches over us when we are weak He is always there to convict, guide, renew and strengthen us.

Think about this scripture, it is the key to your power with God:

> *Isaiah 40:31, "But they that wait upon the Lord shall renew their strength; they shall mount up with wings as eagles; they shall run, and not be weary; and they shall walk, and not faint."*

JESUS HAS EQUIPPED HIS MINISTERS AND HIS CHURCH IN THESE LAST DAYS!

Christ Jesus has given perfect provisions to His people. He has given the Holy Spirit's anointing with power to resist and overcome the devil's attacks. This is His Promise and His Commitment to us.

> *Acts 1:8, "But ye shall receive power, after that the Holy Ghost is come upon you: and ye shall be witnesses unto Me both in Jerusalem, and in all Judea, and in Samaria, and unto the uttermost part of the earth."*

> *John 14:13, "And whatsoever ye shall ask in My Name, that will I do, that the Father may be gloried in the Son."*

HE HAS GIVEN: "THE MINISTRY GIFTS" TO HIS CHURCH!

The ministry gifts Jesus gave to the church are for equipping God's people for service; and for the spiritual growth and development of the body of Christ, as God intended.

> *Ephesians 4:11-14, "And He gave some, apostles; and some, prophets; and some, evangelists; and some, pastors and teachers;"*
>
> *V12, "For the perfecting of the saints, for the work of the ministry, for the edifying of the body of Christ:"*
>
> *V13, "Till we all come in the unity of the faith, and of the knowledge of the Son of God, unto a perfect man, unto the measure of the stature of the fullness of Christ:"*
>
> *V14, "That we henceforth <u>be no more children, tossed to and fro, and carried about with every wind of doctrine,</u> by the sleight of men, and cunning craftiness, whereby they lie in wait to deceive;"*

HE HAS GIVEN "SPIRITUAL GIFTS" TO OPERATE IN HIS CHURCH AND THROUGH BELIEVERS!

Definitions from notes in the Full Life Study Bible

The term Spiritual gifts, refers to supernatural manifestations which comes as gifts from the Holy Spirit operating through believers for the common good.

The purpose of these gifts is to manifest the grace, power, and love of the Holy Spirit among God's people, to be used in public gatherings, churches, families and in our individual lives.

To meet human needs, to strengthen, perfect and build up spiritually both the church and individual believers,

To wage effective spiritual warfare against Satan and the forces of evil:

There are nine Spiritual Gifts given to the church and believers, they are listed in:

1 Corinthians 12:8-11,

"For to one is given by the Spirit: The Word of Wisdom;
To another The Word of Knowledge by the same Spirit;
To another Faith by the same Spirit;
To another the Gifts of Healing by the same Spirit;
To another the Working of Miracles;
To another Prophecy;
To another Discerning of Spirits;
To another Divers Kinds of Tongues;
To another Interpretation of Tongues;
But all these worketh that one and selfsame Spirit, "dividing to every man severally as He will."
These Spiritual Gifts are to be in operation in His church today.

HE HAS GIVEN: "THE FRUIT OF THE SPIRIT" TO INFLUENCE AND DIRECT OUR LIVES!

Galatians 5:22-23, 25, "But the Fruit of the Spirit is: love, joy, peace, longsuffering, gentleness, goodness, faith, meekness, temperance against such there is no law."

V25, "If we live in the Spirit, let us also walk in the Spirit."

Definitions from notes in the Full Life Study Bible

The fruit of the Spirit is produced in God's children as we allow the Spirit to direct and influence our lives that they destroy the power of sin, especially the works of flesh and to walk in fellowship with God.

THE FRUIT OF THE SPIRIT IS:

LOVE: Caring and seeking for the highest good of another person without motive for personal gain.

JOY: The feeling of gladness based on the love, grace, blessings, promises and nearness of God that belongs to believes in Christ.

PEACE: The quietness of heart and mind based on the knowledge that all is well between the believer and our heavenly Father.

LONGSUFFERING: Endurance, patience, being slow to anger or despair.

GENTLENESS: Not wanting to hurt someone or give them pain.

GOODNESS: A zeal for truth and righteousness and a hatred for evil. It can be expressed in acts of kindness, or in rebuking and correcting evil.

FAITH: Faithfulness, firm and unswerving loyalty to one united by promise, commitment, trustworthiness and honesty.

MEEKNESS: restraint with strength and courage; describes a person who can be angry when anger is needed, and humbly submissive when submission is needed.

TEMPERANCE: having control over ones' own desires, passions, and purity.

HE HAS GIVEN "THE WHOLE ARMOR OF GOD" THAT WE MAY BE ABLE TO STAND AGAINST THE WILES OF THE DEVIL!

Ephesians 6:10-19, "Finally, my brethren, be strong in the Lord, and in the power of His might."

V11, "Put on the whole armor of God, that ye may be able to stand against the wiles of the devil."

V12, "For we wrestle not against flesh and blood, but against principalities, against powers, and the rulers of the darkness of this world, against spiritual wickedness in high places."

V13, "Wherefore take unto you the whole armor of God that ye may be able to withstand in the evil day and having done all, to STAND."

V14, "STAND THEREFORE, having your loins girt about with truth, and having on the breastplate of righteousness;"

V15, "And your feet shod with the preparation of the Gospel of peace;"

V16, "Above all, taking the shield of faith, wherewith ye shall be able to quench all the fiery darts of the wicked."

V17, "And take the helmet of salvation, and the sword of the Spirit, which is the Word of God:"

V18, "Praying always with all prayer and supplication in the Spirit, and watching thereunto with all perseverance and supplication for all saints;"

V19, "And for me that utterance may be given unto me, that I may open my mouth boldly, to make known the mystery of the Gospel."

WAKE UP CHURCH!
WAKE UP CHRISTIANS!

Romans 13:11, "And that, knowing the time, that now <u>it is high time to awake out of sleep:</u> for now is our salvation nearer than when we believed."

V12, "The night is far spent, the day is at hand: <u>let us therefore cast off the works of darkness, and let us put on the armor of light."</u>

Many Christians are struggling under the circumstances that surround them. Others have been lulled to sleep spiritually! We are exposed to works of darkness meant to deceive, discourage, and rob us of morals and values and our Spiritual peace and joy.

Take heart, revival is in the air! God is pouring out His spirit on all who hunger for the outpouring of the old time Pentecostal fire of the Holy Spirit to burn in our lives and our churches.

Returning to the old paths, old fashioned prayer meetings, and repentance will help dispel doubts and fears, inspire and renew confidence, faith and trust in God, His Word and His Promises.

In the Name of Jesus we will defeat the Devil and he will flee from us.

He will be the one to shake and tremble in fear because as Spirit filled Christians:

We are the devil's worst nightmare! Because:
We are the Called, Chosen and Commissioned.
We are the Blood Bought Church of Jesus the Christ
We are Spirit filled believers: on fire for God
We are alive and well
We are Victorious Over-comers
We are made more than Conquerors!

MORE THAN A CONQUOR

2 Timothy 1:12, "For the which cause I also suffer these things: <u>nevertheless I am not ashamed: for I know Whom I have believed, and am persuaded that He is able to keep that which I have committed unto Him against that day."</u>

In, 1 Samuel Chapter 17, his brothers made fun of David when he told them he would kill the giant. Little David armed only with five smooth stones and a sling shot faces his Goliath, the champion of the Philistines. He places one stone in his slingshot swings it around.

1 Samuel 17:45-46, "Then said David to the Philistine, "Thou comest to me with a sword, and with a spear, and with a shield: <u>but I come to thee in the Name of the Lord of Hosts, the God of the Armies of Israel, Whom thou hast defiled."</u>

V46, "This day: will the Lord deliver thee into mine hand; and I will smite thee, and take thine head from thee; and I will give the carcasses of the host of the Philistines this day to the fowls of the air, and to the wild beasts of the earth; <u>that all the earth may know that: THERE IS A GOD IN ISRAEL."</u>

When David let loose of the slingshot, he released his faith and confidence in God, and, that nine foot tall warrior giant, champion of their enemy fell to the ground dead. David stands on the giant's chest, takes the giants own sword and whacks off his head.

He had already conquered Goliath, but when he whacked off the giant's head, he was more than a conqueror.

JESUS HAS EQUIPPED US TO BE MORE THAN CONQUERORS.

1 Timothy 6:12, (We are to) "Fight the good fight of faith, lay hold on eternal life, whereunto thou art also "CALLED", and hast professed a good profession before many witnesses."

2 Timothy 2:4, "No man that warreth, entangleth himself with the affairs of this life; that he may please Him who hath "CHOSEN" him to be a soldier."

Luke 10:17, (Jesus sent out the seventy,) "And the seventy returned again with joy saying, Lord, even the devils are subject unto us through Thy Name."

Luke 10:19-20, Jesus said, "Behold, I give unto you power to tread on serpents and scorpions, and over ALL the power of the enemy: and NOTHING shall by any means hurt you."

V20, "Notwithstanding in this, rejoice not, that the spirits are subject unto you; but rather rejoice, because your names are written in heaven."

NOTHING SHALL SEPARATE US FROM THE LOVE OF CHRIST

Romans 8:35, 37-39, V35 "Who shall separate us from the Love of Christ? Shall tribulation, or distress, or persecution, or famine, or nakedness, or peril, or sword?"

V37, "Nay, in <u>all</u> these things <u>we are more than conquerors</u> through Him that loved us."

V38, <u>"For I am persuaded,</u> that neither death, nor life, nor angels, nor principalities, nor powers, nor things present, nor things to come,"

V 39, "Nor height, nor depth, nor any other creature, <u>shall be able to separate us from the Love of God, which is in Christ Jesus, our Lord."</u>

"THIS GOSPEL SHALL BE PREACHED"

Matthew 24:14 "And this gospel of the kingdom shall be preached in all the world for a witness unto all nations; and then shall the end come."

Romans 10:13-15, V13, "For whosoever shall call upon the Name of the Lord shall be saved."

V14, "How then shall they call on Him in Whom they have not believed? And how shall they believe in Him of Whom they have not heard? And how shall they hear without a preacher?"

V15, "And how shall they preach, except they be sent? As it is written: How beautiful are the feet of them that preach the Gospel of peace, and bring glad tidings and good things!"

THINK ON THIS!

Every lost person is a captive of Satan, who seeks to keep them bound in their sin to live as his captives. Their destiny is an eternal hell. The battle for the souls of all mankind *rages*.

We stand in the gap and make up the hedge on behalf of lost souls. Jesus bought and paid the supreme sacrifice for the souls of all mankind at Calvary. He reveals His purpose, and His promise in Luke Chapter 4.

> *Luke 4:18-19, V18, "The Spirit of the Lord is upon Me, because, He hath anointed Me to preach the Gospel to the poor, He hath sent Me to heal the brokenhearted, to preach deliverance to the captives, and recovering of sight to the blind, to set at liberty them that are bruised,"*
>
> *V19, "To preach the acceptable year of the Lord."*
>
> *V21, "This day is this scripture fulfilled in your ears."*

Preachers, Preacher's wives, Women in Ministries, Missionaries, Evangelists, Bible Teachers, Music and Worship Ministers and Spiritual Leaders in Christian Ministries, and Believers:

YOU ARE:
THE CALLED,
THE CHOSEN AND,
THE COMMISSIONED

JESUS LEFT THESE INSTRUCTIONS FOR YOU, HIS MINISTERS AND HIS CHURCH

John 14.12
"Verily, Verily, I Say Unto You:
He that believeth on me,
The works that I do, shall he do also"
And greater works than these shall he do
Because I go to My Father."

ALL THESE THINGS MAKE UP:

THE PURPOSE OF THE CALL!

THE CALLING

A Poem written by Reverend Darrell G Kirk. As a Church of God Holiness Minister, he pastored for over forty years, ministered in Christian Schools, as principle, and teacher. This poem is from his book "Poetry of life". Used by permission.

THE CALLING

We Christians have a calling,
From darkness unto light,
Into God's Great salvation,
Away from sin's dark night

We have a wondrous calling,
That is from God above,
To share His glorious Gospel,
And show His precious love.

We have a wondrous calling,
Which we must never shun,
So many are lost and dying,
Their souls must now be won.

The time is for all Christians,
To understand their call,
We cannot sit by idle,
But, give to God our all.

You see it's so important,
That we all do our part,
To bring the lost to Jesus,
To cleanse the sinful heart,

So, do not be discouraged,
But, just keep pressing on,
And live for Jesus daily,

UNTIL OUR WORK IS DONE!

ACKNOWLEDGMENTS

Thanks to family and friends who encouraged me to write this book. Especially my Pastor, and Pastor's Wife, Reverend Tony and Janie Minick and my loving church family at River of Life Assembly of God in Mabelvale, Arkansas, who encourages, and prays for me daily.

Special thanks to: The ministers and minister's wives who have opened their hearts and shared their experiences in this book.

They are well known and most are credential ministers in their own right. May you be blessed and enjoy each of their experiences shared, especially a young Missionary Child, Miss Shirleyna Jackson who was five years old at that time.

Thanks to each of the Women of God, who shared Words of Wisdom from their hearts in this book, they are:

Mrs. Alton (Johanna) Garrison
Mrs. Don (Martha) Tennison
Mrs. Larry (Judy) Moore
Mrs. Glenn (Debbie) Young
Mrs. Matthew (Stephanie) Hodges
Mrs. Bill (Patty) Hogan Hughart
Mrs. Cecil (Teena) Whaley Culbreth
Mrs. Dean (Peggy) Caldwell
Mrs. Scott (Trudy) Jackson
Miss Shirleyna Jackson
Mrs. Bob (Wanda) Huie

Mrs. Tommy (Jane) Powell Carpenter
Miss Nadine Waldrop
Mrs. Bobby L. (Pam) Johnson
Mrs. Laron (Barbara) Blann
Mrs. Thomas (Angelia) Carpenter

And a poem "The Calling" by
Reverend Darrell G. Kirk

APPENDIX 1

Scriptures listed by chapter, are written in King James Version. Unless otherwise noted.

Introduction: Rev.17:14.

Chapter 1, So, You Are A Woman In The Ministry
2 Co. 12:9; 1 Co. 12:11; 1 Co. 9:27; Lu. 1:26-38; Lu. 1:28, 30; 2 Co. 12:10; 1 Pe. 4:12-14; Ro. 10:14-15; Phm. 4:11; He. 13:5; Je. 29:11-13.

Chapter 2, Protect Your Ministry And Your Marriage
Ex. 17:8-13; Mt. 21:13-14; 1 Th. 5:22-23; 1 Ti. 5:8; Ep. 4:26-27; Mk. 11:26; Ac. 6:3-7.

Chapter 3, Where He Leads, I Will Follow
1 K. 17:2-10; Da. 10:13; Is. 65:24; Jud. 6:36-39; Jn.10:3-5; Ro. 8:28; Ps. 91; Mt. 4:6; Lu. 4:10-11; Ac. 14:27; Jn. 10:7, 9; 2 Co. 2:12; Col. 4:3; Re. 3:8; Ex. 14:14; 2 Chr. 20:15, 17; 2 Chr. 32:7-8; Je. 29:11-14.

Chapter 4, Never A Dull Moment In The Parsonage
1Co. 9:23-27; Ps. 19:14; Pr. 15:1-2; Ex. 32:7, 11; Mt. 10:16; 1 Pe. 5:8; Lu. 10:19; Jn. 14:12-18.

Chapter 5, Raising Awesome Godly Preacher's Kids
Mk. 10:13-16; Pr. 13:24; Ac.17; Is. 54:17; Mt. 5:14-16;

Ep. 6:10-20; Ps. 91:9-12,14,15; De. 6:5-9; Pr. 22:6; Lu. 11:1;
Lu. 18:16; 1 S. 3:10-20; 1 Co. 6:9-10; 1 Co. 6:18-20;
Ps. 91:9-11; Ac. 19:11-12; Heb. 12:15; Prov. 22:6; De. 6:4-9;
Pr.22:6.

Chapter 6, Dealing With Difficult Situations
Ps. 23:1-6; Ac.9:15; Ps. 17:8; Ps, 30:5; Prov. 15:1; Ro. 16:17-20;
Mk. 11:25-26; Ro. 12:20-21; Is. 53:3-5; Jn. 1:10-12; Prov. 15:1;
Ps, 105:14-15; Mk. 5 & 6; Mk. 6:31-32; 1 Pe. 4:12-13;
1 Pe. 3 & 4; Ex. 33:18, 21-22; Je. 33:3.

Chapter 7, My House Shall Be A House Of Hospitality.
Rom. 16:17-18; Mt. 16:18-19 Mt. 6:6; Eph. 6:10-20.

Chapter 8, Fear Faith And Trust
2 Ti. 1:7; Lu. 22:31-32; Ro. 8:34-39; Ac. 27:22-25; Ac. 28:3-6;
Ps. 91:11; 2 K. 6:12; 2 K. 6:15-20; 2 Ti. 1:7-14; Is. 65:24;
Ac. 16:22-36; Is. 12:2-6.

Chapter 9, Words Of Wisdom
Ps. 1:3; 2 Co. 2:15; (NLT); Ep. 5:1-2; (NLT); 2 Co. 2:15;
(NLT) Mk. 11:26; De. 6:4-9; Is. 54:13; De. 6:5; Eph. 6:1; Is. 11:6;
Pr. 22:6; Ru. Chapters 1-4; De. 23:21-23; Ps.34:18-19;
Pr. 18:21; Ps. 46:10; Rom. Read Chapter 5.

Chapter 10, Purpose Of The Call
Ge. 12:1; Mt. 22:37-38; Ac. 26:16; 1 Pe. 5:2; Ac 20:28; Mt. 10:16;
2 Tim. 1:7; Ep. 6:16; Ro. 12:3; Mt. 10:1; 2 Co. 10:4-5; 1 Pe.5:8-11;
Is. 40:31; Ac. 1:8; Jn. 14:13; Eph. 4:11-14; 1 Co. 12:8-11;
Ga. 5:22-23, 25; Ep. 6:10-19; Ro. 13:11-12; 2Ti. 1:12;
1 S. 17:45-46; 1 Ti. 6:12; 2 Ti. 2:4; Lu. 10:17, 19-20;
Ro. 8:35, 37-39; Mt. 24:14; Rom. 10:13-15; Lu. 4:18-19, 21;
Jn. 14:12.

CPSIA information can be obtained
at www.ICGtesting.com
Printed in the USA
LVHW081023100821
694457LV00008B/15

9 781478 794271